JESUS IS HERE

Also by Father Myers:

The Book of Mary
Journal of a Parish Priest
Lent: A Journey to Resurrection

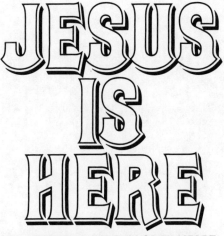

JESUS IS HERE

DEVOTIONS TO THE SACRED HEART AND PRECIOUS BLOOD

Rawley Meyers

Our Sunday Visitor Publishing Division
Our Sunday Visitor, Inc.
Huntington, Indiana 46750

Our Sunday Visitor Publishing Division
Our Sunday Visitor, Inc., 200 Noll
Plaza, Huntington, IN 46750

Library of Congress Catalog Card Number: 85-63066
International Standard Book Number: 0-87973-520-1

Cover design by James E. McIlrath

Printed in the United States of America

To
ARCHBISHOP JAMES V. CASEY
of Denver
with admiration
and gratitude

Contents

Introduction

Jesus is everything. The whole of Christianity is to know Christ Jesus. And the more we know him, the more we love him and will follow him. To follow Jesus is joy.

One of the most beautiful teachings of Jesus is that we are not alone. He is with us always and everywhere. He promised, "Behold, I am with you always, even until the end of the world." Jesus is beside us, here and now, to help us on our journey to heaven. How gracious he is. If we never lose sight of him we will always be happy, even in the midst of adversity.

One of the saints asked, "Are you not Christ's purchased possession?" Christ, who suffered so much for you, loves you with all his heart. We belong to him; on the cross he purchased heaven for us. He wishes to repeat in each of us the figure of himself, who "went about doing good." That is what it means to be a Christian, a Christ-follower.

Man can stop loving God, but God can never stop loving us. His love is too great for that. He sent His Son to rescue us from our selfishness. Jesus is our Savior. He became a castaway for our sake, to restore us as children of God. Because His Son humbled himself, God exalted us. The merits of Christ are the cause of our sanctification and of the innumerable graces showered upon us. We should be filled with unutterable gratitude.

Jesus came to infuse life into our souls, to receive the wayward back into the love of his heart. Let us then determine all the more to pursue him. For Jesus said,

"Whoever believes in the Son has everlasting life." And
St. Paul said of Christ, "Whoever believes in him shall
not be confounded." In our age of cynicism and skepticism, we need a greater faith in Jesus; we need to know
Christ more, for as St. Peter assures us, by believing we
shall "rejoice with joy unspeakable."

RAWLEY MYERS

I. JUNE: Month of the Sacred Heart

O Sacred Heart of Jesus.
I put all my trust in you.

During June, through these daily readings and prayers, we reflect on the tremendous love that the Sacred Heart of Jesus has for each one of us.

11

June Devotions

Reflection for June 1

Jesus asked to be baptized, but John said, "I ought to be baptized by you, and you ask me to baptize you?" Jesus replied, "Let us do it this way for now so that all things will be fulfilled." Archbishop Fulton Sheen said that Jesus asked for baptism "in order to identify himself with sinful humanity," whom he was to redeem. He who called himself the Son of Man had for his mission the salvation of mankind. He wished to save us all. Jesus was indeed to be the "Lamb of God" who, like the sacrificial lamb offered in the Temple, would be killed for the sins of the people.

Christ's divine mission was confirmed after his baptism. As he came out of the water, the Holy Spirit in the form of a dove rested on him and a voice came from heaven saying, "This is my beloved Son in whom I am well pleased."

Then the Spirit drove Jesus into the desert. There he fasted and prayed, living in a cave among the wild beasts. St. James wrote, "Blessed is he who endures under trial and has proved his worth." And so after forty days in the desert, Jesus was tempted by Satan. The Prince of Darkness told him that if he would give up his messianic mission he would be given great earthly power and tremendous popularity and a life of pleasure. Most men find these temptations too heady to refuse. Our pride seeks such things with a passion. But Jesus would not budge, even though the Devil warned him that his

way of humility and servitude leads to death. Sneered
Satan: "Humans cannot stand good for long, and they
soon get rid of the good man." All this Jesus knew, but he
still stood firm.

He endured the temptations to show us that God
makes His loved ones perfect through trial and suffering.

(Recite one of the June prayers beginning on
page 49.)

Reflection for June 2

Man is buffeted all his days by temptations of the
kind that Jesus endured. The evil one tried to win him by
pretending that he wanted to help him: he offered evil
disguised as good. Satan proposed, first of all, social reform as a way for Jesus to win men over. Give the people
bread, and they will follow you. Why should Jesus suffer,
and why should he let others suffer? Do away with pain —
aren't so many of our TV commercials saying the same?
But Jesus knew Satan was trying to tempt him away
from the cross, just as later men would cry on Calvary,
"Come down from the cross and we will believe you."
Christ's reply was his classic statement, "Man does not
live by bread alone." Jesus said in effect, "You want me
to fill men's bellies instead of their souls. I don't want to
make men richer; I want to make them holier."

The second temptation by the Devil was directed to
vanity. Do something spectacular, put on a circus act,
and great crowds of curiosity seekers will come out to
see you, he told Jesus. Give up this silly idea of suffering
for the people; do some daring deed to attract them.

But Jesus knew that though stunts and tricks
fascinate many people, mobs like that do not listen. Jesus
wanted to teach the people, to tell his vital message, to

win hearts. Love was his weapon. He would not tempt God for "special effects."

In the third temptation, Jesus was offered a great kingdom if he would bow to Satan. But the answer of Christ foreshadowed his words to Pilate, "My kingdom is not of this world." And he said, "Begone, Satan!"

Some today try to mock the Gospels and tell us there is no Devil, precisely what Satan wants us to believe. But there is too much evil in the world to deny its source. Satan is never more active and insidious than when he is spreading the rumor that he does not exist.

Jesus was severely tempted, and therefore he is never insensitive to our temptations. In the words of the Letter to the Hebrews, "We have not a high priest who cannot have compassion on our infirmities, but one tempted in all things as we are, without sin."

(Recite one of the June prayers.)

Reflection for June 3

Jesus triumphed over the temptations of the Devil in the desert and then returned to the towns of men, where he began to speak in the various villages of Galilee. Whenever and wherever he spoke, he touched hearts. People said in amazement, "No man ever spoke like this man." Jesus stretched out his sacred hands and healed people in soul and body. The crowds marveled; they praised him for his wisdom and his goodness. He so far surpassed any other teacher that some would not believe. His message simply seemed too marvelous, "too good to be true." It is hard for suspicious, skeptical humans to believe in the great and overwhelming generosity of God. Others, however, were more open. To them, what Jesus said was joy, like water in the thirsty desert. What he proclaimed was what their hearts had been looking for all their lives.

Then one day Jesus returned to his hometown of Nazareth. He wanted to tell his own people the "good news." He sought to relate to them the Fatherhood of God and the happiness of serving Him.

It was the Sabbath, and the people, as was their custom, assembled in the synagogue. Nazareth was a small town and had no rabbi, no Scripture teacher, so anyone could get up and speak about the holy books.

Jesus asked the clerk for the sacred manuscripts rolled up in scrolls. The attendant drew aside the silk curtain of the painted Ark of the Covenant and Jesus took out the writings of the Prophet Isaiah. He unrolled it to the sixty-first chapter, which foretold the great day of mercy when the Messiah would come. All the Jewish nation longed for this much-desired person, to be sent by God, who would break the chains of slavery to sin and heal the wounded world.

Jesus read the Messianic prophecy of Isaiah and then stated solemnly that this day the prophecy was fulfilled. He was the one sent from God to proclaim the way of God. The people were amazed. They could not believe their ears. His message was so sublime that they thrilled at the beautiful words he spoke, but they had seen Jesus grow up in their midst and become their carpenter like his father, Joseph. They would not believe in him.

(Recite one of the June prayers.)

Reflection for June 4

Jesus was disappointed in Nazareth. He had a special love for his hometown people, and he wanted to help them most of all, but they would not accept him. When he saw their lack of faith, he said, "A prophet is honored everywhere but in his own hometown." He told them they were no better than their forefathers who had stoned and killed the ancient prophets. This made some of the hotheads in the crowd angry, and they grabbed him and took him out to a cliff to do him in.

Jesus, they said, could not possibly be the Great One, for he had been a workman in their village. Hadn't they seen him day after day bent over his carpenter's bench, toiling like everyone else? They had known him as a boy when his good mother sent him on errands of mercy, taking bread and soup to the sick.

On the hill, however, the hotheads could not do anything. While Jesus stood there calmly, almost majestically, a noble figure, his dark eyes piercing them through, no one in the crowd could move. Indeed no man who saw his look that day ever forgot it. No one dared touch him. And Jesus walked through the crowd and down the hill and left Nazareth.

He went to the nearby Galilean village of Capernaum on the shores of the Sea of Galilee. He never returned to Nazareth — to these people who did not have faith — except to pass through.

In Capernaum he also taught in the synagogue on the Sabbath, and the people "were astonished at his teaching, for his word was spoken with authority." Unlike the other Jewish religious teachers who were forever quoting someone else, Jesus spoke a sublime message in his own name. They never had heard words like his before, and never would hear such words again.

One day while the crowds were pressing upon him to hear him, he was standing on the beach by the Sea of Galilee and he saw a boat with the fishermen washing their nets. Jesus got into a boat belonging to Simon (Peter) and asked him to put out a little from the shore. Sitting in the boat, he taught the people.

(Recite one of the June prayers.)

Reflection for June 5

After Jesus had preached in the boat, he told Simon to push out into the deep and he would make a catch. Simon replied, "Master, we have labored the whole night and have taken nothing. But at your word I will go out and lower my net." And when he did so, the net was filled with fish. Seeing this, Simon fell on his knees before Jesus and said, "Depart from me, O Lord, for I am a sinful man." But Jesus replied, "Do not be afraid. From henceforth I will make you a fisher of men."

Not long after, Jesus was walking along the beach near the boats and he saw Simon, Andrew, James, and John mending their nets. He said, "Come, follow me." And they left everything and followed him. They did not know where they were going or what they were to do, but they wanted to be with him. Jesus does that to people. To be with him makes one feel that all else is like nothing. In exchange for trinkets, Jesus wants to give us himself. Christianity is truly the pauper becoming a prince. Christ invites us to throw away our crust of bread and join him in a great banquet.

The disciples asked Jesus where he was going. He said simply, "Come and see." And they went with him. Once we love Jesus, we too must go with him. At the invitation of Jesus, the Apostles were confused; so are we. They were slow of mind and heart; we are more so. They followed Jesus not knowing why; we don't know any more. All we know is what they seemed to sense: that every step toward Jesus is a step toward God and His home in heaven.

When the Apostles followed Jesus, who himself is the Way, they found Love. They went with him and discovered, as we do, that he is a most gracious host. In our darkness, we see so little of life and even less of the future. But if we walk with Jesus, he will guide us.

Christ says to us, "Come and see." If we do go with him then we will come to see; we'll see the vanity of earthly pursuits, the futility of trying to make a paradise on earth. We'll see that with Jesus we are surrounded by mercy, sanctified by the sacraments, and given more graces. We see the shamefulness of sin, but, even more, we see the boundlessness of the love of Christ.

After the first disciples spent a day with Jesus, they could not spend a day without him.

(Recite one of the June prayers.)

Reflection for June 6

Jesus passed by Levi, who was sitting in his tax collector's booth. He had passed by him before and had seen his doglike eyes follow him. This time Jesus said, "Follow me." Levi's heart filled with love; he could not explain why. He stood up and left his lucrative labor to go with Jesus. That night Levi (later called Matthew) gave a banquet for Jesus. Since tax collectors were so hated, he had no friends but other tax collectors, and they were all invited. Looking in at the dinner, the Pharisees, the Jewish religious leaders and teachers, immediately grumbled at what they saw. They said that this Jesus surely could not be a good man if he would eat with sinners. But Jesus replied, "This is why I have come — for sinners." He said people don't blame a doctor for being with sick people — that is his calling, so why blame Jesus for being with the spiritually sick? To save them was his mission. "I have come," he said, "not to call the righteous but to call sinners to repentance."

Jesus gathered twelve disciples around him. They were his favorite friends and were called the Apostles. These men heard him speak and he did so in a way they had never heard before. They were not brilliant men; in fact, for the most part, just the opposite; but when he told of the "good news" that he had brought to man, it moved them in a way they had never been moved before. Ever after, they walked with him. Often they could not understand him, but they could not leave him.

However, while the Apostles admired him with all their hearts, another group, the Pharisees, much more powerful, opposed him. Deep down they were jealous of him. They were supposed to be the religious leaders and teachers, but here the large crowds were going out to hear Jesus. They envied him so much they could hardly stand it. They loved to have people bowing to them and kissing their hands and bringing them gifts. Now this upstart from a small village in rural Galilee, without any real schooling, was preaching and the people flocked to him. The Pharisees simply must put a stop to it.

(Recite one of the June prayers.)

Reflection for June 7

Jesus, with some of the Apostles, was invited to a marriage feast at Cana. Mary was there. And after a time Mary went to her Son and said, "They have no wine." How disgraced this young newlywed couple would be if they ran out of refreshments for their guests. A wedding day is supposed to be one of happy memories, not a day of humiliation like this.

Mary saw all this, and like a mother she sought to do something. Among Jewish people in particular, hospitality is of paramount importance. She spoke to Jesus of the sad situation. She said little, but they knew each other so well he understood what she wanted. He knew too that she had always taught him, "We are not for ourselves but for others."

Nevertheless Jesus was reluctant. He was not yet ready to work a public miracle and step into the spotlight on center stage. He had intended to unfold his teaching gradually, so as slowly to prepare the people for his heavenly message. But because Mary asked him, all was changed. He denied himself his own desires and worked the miracle she wanted. And by changing the water into wine for the guests, Jesus enabled the gladness of the feast to go on.

Jesus wishes to change us also, to take away our sins, the source of our despair. With his divine love, he is always pleading with us, seeking to come into our hearts and bring his peace and happiness. The God of all consolation knocks daily at the door of our hearts, his arms loaded with gifts.

Yes, Jesus wishes to come in. Open the door wide. Jesus is the best of company. As at the marriage feast, he comes and cheers us and celebrates with us and changes the water of our sadness into the wine of joy. Do not be afraid to invite him in. It will be the best thing you do in your whole life. He will add greatly to your happiness, as he did at the marriage feast at Cana.

(Recite one of the June prayers.)

Reflection for June 8

Jesus began now to work many miracles to help heal people in body and soul. Luke tells us of one afternoon: "Now when the sun was setting, all who had sick with various diseases brought them to him. And he laid his hands upon each of them and cured them." He helped all who came to him.

One day he was teaching in a house, and some men carried up a friend who was paralyzed. Because of the crowd they could not enter through the door. Jewish houses, however, had an outside stairway and a flat roof that was used as a porch, a place to catch the breeze and cool off after the desert sun went down. Too, the houses had a skylight to let in light and heat; they were too poor, of course, for glass, so it was covered with straw.

The friends took the paralyzed man up on the roof and pulled back the straw matting and with ropes let down the stretcher to the feet of Christ. Jesus looked into the eyes of the man and saw his faith. He said, "Be of good heart, son, your sins are forgiven you."

The nearby Pharisees were horrified and whispered to one another, "This is blasphemy, for only God can forgive sins." Of course, they were right, and Jesus did not deny it. But to prove that he had this divine power, Jesus said, "Which is easier for me to do, heal you in soul or heal you in body? But to show that I can heal you in soul, I will heal you in body." And he said, "Take up you stretcher and go home." And the man did so. "And astonishment seized them all, and they glorified God and were filled with fear, saying 'We have seen wonderful things today.' "

The Pharisees and the other religious leaders opposed Jesus here because they were jealous of him. They wanted at first to discredit him, and so sought to make him look foolish before the people. But each time they tried, they fell into their own trap.

(Recite one of the June prayers.)

Reflection for June 9

Especially were the Pharisees enraged when Jesus told the people that these leaders were proud and petty and even wrong at times. It is very dangerous to contradict or criticize a proud person. The Pharisees fumed. They deeply resented his remarks and said he was ruining the people. He continued, however, to point out the stupidity of their merciless literalness and their ill-inspired zeal for their own importance. He told them to their faces that they poisoned their teaching with pride. In great anger the leaders struck out in all directions, determined to destroy him by fair means or foul.

At first the Pharisees thought they could show him up with trick questions. After all, he had never been to school. But every trick question backfired. They sought to make him out to be a fool and they ended up looking like fools themselves.

Jesus said they were hard of heart and blindly obstinate. The love of God was a strong love, but they had buried it in formalism. They were defeating themselves and dragging down the people with them, and they were supposed to be leading them upward to God.

The hostile Pharisees, failing to trap him with questions, became even more determined to get him out of the way. They kept saying it was for the good of the people; they never dared mention that they longed again for the admiration of the crowds. No wonder the people turned to Christ. He held out hope and salvation to every-

one; the Pharisees piled on a thousand rules. As if in
proof of what he said of their pride, it was impossible for
them to conceal their hatred for him. They were insane
with rage, and they decided on more extreme measures.
They found they could not win an argument with him, for
they would offer a ponderous question with weighty
words and Jesus responded with lightning-like clarity.
The people enjoyed these exchanges and Jesus became
more popular than ever, while the fuming Pharisees
grew more embarrassed.

(Recite one of the June prayers.)

Reflection for June 10

Jesus preached so beautifully. In his first recorded
talk outdoors, the Sermon on the Mount, he mentioned
the Beatitudes.

It was early morning and already the people were
coming. The dark, steep hills beyond the lake were beginning to reflect the sunlight. Jesus had prayed the
whole night; this often was his custom. Now near mid-
morning, people gathered all over the hill to hear him.
He spoke and said, "Blessed are the poor in spirit, for
theirs is the kingdom of heaven. Blessed are the meek,
for they shall possess the land. Blessed are they who
mourn, for they shall be comforted. Blessed are they who
hunger and thirst for justice, for they shall be satisfied.
Blessed are the pure of heart, for they shall see God.
Blessed are the peacemakers, for they shall be called the
children of God. Blessed are they who suffer persecution
for justice, for they shall be greatly rewarded in the kingdom of heaven."

His golden words echoed out across the hills, words

such as humans had never heard before or would hear again.

Jesus said, "You are the salt of the earth, but if the salt loses its flavor, what is it good for? It is no longer of any use but to be thrown out and trodden underfoot."

He went on: "You are the light of the world. Men do not light lamps and put them under a bushel basket. They light lamps to set on the table so all can see. Let others see your works and give glory to your Father in heaven."

Christ continued telling the people that he had come not to destroy the old law but to perfect it and build upon it. He spoke out against hostility: "If you are offering a gift at the altar and remember that your brother has something against you, leave the gift and go first and be reconciled with your brother." He said, "If someone strikes you on the cheek, turn the other cheek; if someone needs your tunic, give him your cloak as well; if someone wants you to go a mile, go two miles with him."

(Recite one of the June prayers.)

Reflection for June 11

"Love your enemies, pray for those who persecute and speak evil of you," Jesus said.

His words were beautiful but were not accepted by all. Predictably the Pharisees were petty, twisting his meaning, unable to see good in anything he said. But many were moved. Jesus ignored the silliness of the religious leaders and looked to the good will of the common people. He said, "He who has ears to hear, let him hear."

Jesus told them that when you help your neighbor, don't make a big show out of it; give in secret and your heavenly Father who sees in secret will reward you. "Do not let your right hand know what your left hand is doing.''

He warned them to beware of false teachers: ''they come in sheep's clothing, but inwardly are ravenous wolves.''

He said that people do not gather grapes from thorns or figs from thistles. Every good tree bears good fruit and every bad tree bears bad fruit. By their fruit you will know them.

Jesus stated that if they followed his teachings they would build their house on rock, but if they did not, they would be building on sand, and when the storm came, and the wind and the rain, they would beat against the house with the poor foundation and it would fall down in ruins.

The people listened to this sublime teaching. They had never heard anything so wonderful before. Though he spoke for a long time, they were sad when he finished. They could have listened to him forever. It was like being in heaven.

When he went down from the hillside a leper came up to him and called out, ''Master, if you will, you can make me clean.''

Jesus said, ''I will,'' and the man was made clean.

(Recite one of the June prayers.)

Reflection for June 12

''Ask and you shall receive, seek and you shall find, knock and it shall be opened to you,'' Jesus said as he spoke about prayer. He explained that when a son asks for a fish, a father does not give him a serpent; if he asks for bread, he is not handed a stone. If a human father is good in giving his children the gifts they need, how much more will your Father in heaven give good things to those who ask Him.

He warned that prayer alone is not enough. "Not everyone who says, 'Lord, Lord,' shall enter the kingdom of heaven, but he who does the will of my Father shall enter the kingdom of heaven."

"When you pray don't be like the hyprocites who love to pray in public and be praised for their praying," Jesus stated. "When you pray, go into your room and close the door and pray in private." He told them they did not have to use many words in prayer or big words, as if anybody could impress God. And he told them that when they fasted they should be cheerful and pleasant.

"Do not be anxious about life, what to eat, what to drink," he continued. "Look at the birds of the air, they neither sow nor reap nor gather into barns, yet your heavenly Father feeds them. Are you not of much more value than they?"

Jesus stated, "And as for clothing, why do you worry? See the lilies of the field, how they grow; they neither toil nor spin, yet I say to you that not even Solomon in all his glory was arrayed like one of these. But if God so clothes the grass of the field, here today and gone tomorrow, how much more you, O you of little faith.

"Therefore, do not fret over what you will eat or what you will drink or what you will put on. These are the things that the pagans worry about. Your Father knows your needs. Rather, seek first the kingdom of God and His ways and all these things will be given to you.

"Do not be anxious about tomorrow, for tomorrow will have its own worries. Today's troubles are sufficient for today."

(Recite one of the June prayers.)

Reflection for June 13

How wonderful were the words of this man from Nazareth!

He told the people, "Do not lay up for yourselves treasures on earth, where the rust and moth consume, and where thieves break in and steal, but lay up for yourselves treasures in heaven, for where your treasure is, there also is your heart."

He added: "Judge not and you will not be judged." The way you judge others will be the way God will judge you. Don't worry so much about your brother's faults; they are small compared to your own.

Not only did the people marvel at his words, but they stood in awe at his healing powers. He said, "The Son of Man is not come to be served but to serve." And this must be true for his followers as well. "The first shall be last and the last shall be first." "Son of Man" was the name for the Messiah given by Daniel the prophet. He used this often because it best showed that he was a servant and a man who suffered to save mankind.

The people noticed that he never sought his own glorification. He wanted only to teach and help others. Above all, his eyes were fixed on his final destiny.

Jesus, his body hardened by work, loved the outdoors, the hills, the lakes, the wildflowers in bright colors, the songs of birds, the stars like diamonds in the black sky. He frequently rose early to see the splendor of the sunrise in purple and red. Material possessions did not interest him; they were more like junk that cluttered up one's life. His delight was in the grandeur of nature. The outdoors was much more magnificent than man-made palaces.

Every day Jesus made a great impression on the crowd. Just the sight of him gave them hope in their work-weary lives; to hear him was never to forget his golden words. He drew people by his noble appearance, and he held them by his great and heartfelt love.

(Recite one of the June prayers.)

Reflection for June 14

Jesus' presence was like the unfolding of a banner on high. His words amazed people, and his healing awed them. He was a person with power and energy, virility and gentleness. His striking eyes and healthy comeliness made people stop and look at him when he did nothing but walk by.

The Apostles were a problem almost from the beginning. With them he exercised the patience of Job. If he set out to choose the most unlikely men to be the leaders of a great movement, he could not have done a better job. They were slow learners, cowardly, inarticulate, all but hopeless. But maybe all this was planned, to show the world that God can write straight with crooked lines.

The Apostles were frequently bickering, especially about who was the most important, proving they understood almost nothing of what Christ preached. Tirelessly he explained his message to them over and over. Again and again he told them their selfishness was self-defeating and self-destructive.

The Apostles were proud. They gloried in standing beside Jesus when he was so popular with the people. When he worked astounding miracles, they were as eager and enthusiastic as the crowds. But when he warned them that all would not be beautiful, that there were days of darkness and suffering ahead, they did not hear him — they did not want to hear him. Like most of us, they listened only when it was pleasant.

Peter especially was a problem, he who was to be the leader of the Twelve. Once when Jesus stated that in time he must go up to Jerusalem and suffer and die, Peter told him not to say things like that. Jesus answered sharply, "You are talking like Satan; do not tempt me to abandon the mission for which I was sent."

(Recite one of the June prayers.)

Reflection for June 15

To strengthen the leaders among the Apostles for the ordeal that lay ahead, Jesus took Peter, James, and John up to Mt. Tabor, and there the great miracle of the Transfiguration transpired. Peter said with enthusiasm, "Lord, it is good for us to be here. If you will, we will build here three tabernacles, one for you, one for Moses and one for Elijah." But then a cloud overshadowed them and a voice said. "This is my beloved Son in whom I am well pleased. Hear him." The three disciples fell on their faces, exceedingly frightened. But Jesus said, "Get up and do not be afraid." Lifting up their eyes, they saw they were alone. He told them not to tell of this vision until "the Son of Man has risen from the dead."

The Transfiguration was a revelation of Jesus in glory. In heaven we will be like Jesus, the Son of God, for we are the adopted sons of God.

When the crowds came to Jesus soon after, he spoke to them of John the Baptist. Why did you go out to hear him, he asked. "What did you go out to the desert to see? A reed shaken in the wind? But what did you go out to see? A man clothed in soft garments? Behold, those who wear soft garments are in the houses of kings. But what did you go out to see? A prophet? Yes, I tell you, and more than a prophet. This is he of whom the prophets said, 'Behold, I send my messenger before my face, who shall make ready my way before me.' "

Jesus concluded, "Amen, I say to you, there has not arisen among those born of woman anyone greater than John the Baptist."

He spoke of John because the Baptist, in prison in Herod's dungeon, had sent several of his followers to ask Jesus, "Are you he who is to come, or shall we look for another?" Jesus answered, "Go and tell John what you have seen and heard; the blind see, the lame walk, the lepers are cleansed, the deaf hear, the dead arise, and the poor have the Gospel preached to them."

(Recite one of the June prayers.)

Reflection for June 16

A ruler of the synagogue named Jairus fell at the feet of Jesus and pleaded with him, "My daughter is near death. Please come and lay your hand on her that she may be saved and live."

Jesus went with Jairus, while a large crowd followed and pressed in upon him. In the crowd was a woman who had a hemorrhage for twelve years and had spent all her money seeking a cure in vain. She said to herself, "If I can only touch the hem of his cloak, I shall be saved." She reached out and did so, and she felt herself healed.

Jesus, feeling that power had gone forth from him, said, "Who touched me?" The Apostles replied, "In a crowd like this, who can tell?" But the woman summoned all her courage and came forth. Jesus said to her gently, "My daughter, your faith has saved you. You are healed. Go in peace."

Just then the servant of Jairus came up and said that his daughter had died. But Jesus said, "Do not be afraid. Only have faith."

They came to the house, and the people were weeping profusely. Jesus asked, "Why are you crying? The girl is asleep, not dead." They laughed at this foolishness. But Jesus had them leave, and he went into the room where the girl was lying. He said, "My child, I say to you, arise." And she rose up and began to walk. She was twelve years old. All were utterly amazed. And Jesus told them to give her something to eat.

On another occasion some people brought to him a deaf man unable to speak. They asked the Lord to lay his hands upon him. Jesus touched the man's ears and tongue and, looking up to heaven, said, "Be opened." And the man's ears were opened and his tongue was loosed, and he could hear and speak. And the people said, "He has done all things well. He makes the deaf to hear and the mute to speak."

(Recite one of the June prayers.)

Reflection for June 17

All his life Jesus had but one desire. He said, "I seek not my own will, but the will of Him who sent me." The wish of his heart was ever the glory of God.

Jesus told of the love of the Father for the smallest bird and the tiniest flower. There can be no doubt then that He has a very wonderful love for each individual. We should open our hearts to Him so that He can give us His love. He will give us grace enough, more than sufficient, as He gently leads us onward.

Jesus said, "My yoke is easy, my burden light." He

seeks to take away our fear by fixing our gaze on God and His love. Without God, there is only brutal force and slavery in the world. Man so often, in his pride, thinks he can do everything, but this is the certain way to disaster. The history of mankind is a history of Godless wars. Without God, man is bewildered and hopeless; he becomes less than human and turns into a wild animal.

Jesus preached humility. He desperately wants us to pray humbly, to beg God for guidance; otherwise humans will destroy themselves in a terrible tragedy of global suicide. Only God can bring about peace and a better world.

Christ told the people not to exhaust themselves by working merely for this world's goods. Seek first the things of God and you will have all else.

A woman whose daughter had an unclean spirit came and fell on her knees while he was in a house. She was a Gentile, a non-Jew. She besought him to help her daughter.

Jesus, said, however, that he had come for the Jews, the Chosen People, first of all. He must help them now; it would be unfair to take their food from them and give it to others. She replied, "But even the dogs under the table get to eat the crumbs that fall to the floor." Jesus blessed her for her faith and determination, and he told her that her daughter had been cured. When she went home she found her girl was well.

(Recite one of the June prayers.)

Reflection for June 18

Jesus took his disciples aside to rest a while. There he said to them, "Who do men say that I am?" Some said that he was John the Baptist come back to life; others said one of the prophets. Then Jesus said, "But you, who do you say that I am?"

Peter answered, "You are the Christ, the Son of the living God." Jesus said, "Blessed are you, Simon son of Jona, for flesh and blood have not revealed this to you, but my Father in heaven."

Jesus then appointed Peter to be the head of his Church. Peter means "rock." He said, "You are Peter and upon this rock I will build my Church, and the forces of evil will not triumph over it. And I will give you the keys of the kingdom of heaven, and whatever you bind on earth shall be bound in heaven, and whatever you loose on earth shall be loosed in heaven."

On this solemn occasion, Jesus promised that Satan, the Father of Lies, would never so influence the Church as to make it preach falsely in the vital matter of eternal salvation. The Church was founded by Christ to be our sure guide to the gates of heaven.

Another time Jesus and his disciples were going to the village of Naim, and a funeral procession was coming out. They were burying a young man, the only son of a widow. Her tears and sobs were uncontrollable. Jesus, filled with compassion, stopped the procession. He said to the mother, "Do not weep." Then he said, "Young man, I say to you, arise," and the young man did so. And the merciful Jesus gave the boy back to his amazed and grateful mother. The crowd said, "A great prophet has risen among us, and God has visited His people." The report of this event went around the whole countryside.

Jesus was constantly helping the poor people because his heart was full of love.

(Recite one of the June prayers.)

Reflection for June 19

The Roman conquerors of Palestine were harsh and domineering. The Jewish people had lost their heritage during this tragic period in their history.

The crowd who came to hear Jesus was made up for the most part of the poor, the forgotten, the unfortunate. These people could not explain how they knew, but they did know that he had a special love for them. Jesus indeed told them that they were blessed, something he never said to the rich or the Pharisees or the other important people. He gave them hope, these individuals who suffered so much and worked so hard. He said that the gates of heaven would be open to them, and there they would find an existence richer by far than anything we can now dream of. The soul in heaven will be ever refreshed by a new spring of joy. God's home, which will be our home, is a place of inexhaustible happiness and variety and fullness.

Few things are so fatiguing as teaching, answering questions, and explaining again and again. And yet Jesus always responded with gentleness; he was especially kind to sinners.

Jesus said that he was the vine and we are the branches. The branch receives its nourishment and life from the vine. Cut off the branch from the vine and it shrivels up and dies. The branch is not attached to the vine like an ornament to a Christmas tree. It grows from the vine, sharing its life. The energy comes from the vine; the branch is nothing without it. We are nothing without Jesus.

When he was not preaching he was praying, and when he was not praying he was healing. "A great crowd came to him," Matthew writes, "bringing with them the mute, the blind, the lame, the maimed, and many others, and they set them down at his feet, and he cured them.''

Jesus taught that we must show kindness to one another. Loving and helping our neighbor is the way to Christ's heart. We should pray that we see Christ in our neighbor and that charity will leap up within us and pour out upon others.

(Recite one of the June prayers.)

Reflection for June 20

Often, as we know so well, our hearts feel as lifeless as a fountain without water. We must pray for help from Jesus. Christ is the source of love; we must go to him to find the "living water." Without Jesus we remain apathetic and mediocre, but by his merits our love overflows.

To imitate Jesus is not easy. Some begin with intoxicating enthusiasm, but they have no roots, as he told us in the parable, and they do not last. In this story the seed is the word of God. The planter sows the seed. Some falls by the wayside, and the birds come and eat it up. This represents those who do not comprehend Jesus so that it is easy for the enemy to snatch his word out of their hearts. Some seed fell on rocky ground and sprang up quickly but had no roots and was soon scorched by the sun. They are the fair-weather friends, and when trouble comes they fade away.

Some seed fell among thorns and was soon choked off by them. The thorns represent the concerns of the world, which so preoccupy people that they forget about God. But, thank heaven, some seed fell on good ground and produced a rich harvest.

Jesus wanted all to know his message of love. He

knew that without God the light goes out and night falls
and people stumble around in confusion. He wanted to
help them, guard them, guide them. He said, "I am the
light of the world."

The only group to whom he showed anger were the
proud and pompous Pharisees. He hoped that perhaps by
hard words he could break through their hard hearts. He
called them "whited sepulchers." The Jewish people
buried their dead above ground in caves chiseled out of
large boulders, which were then whitewashed to make
them look more attractive. The Pharisees were like that,
Jesus said, pleasant enough looking on the outside — but
inside full of dead men's bones. But even these scathing
denunciations did not touch the hearts of the haughty religious leaders. They continued to be hypercritical and
sneering. They were spiritually blind, so taken up with
their own importance.

(Recite one of the June prayers.)

Reflection for June 21

Jesus finished a discourse in Capernaum when a Roman centurion sent word that his faithful servant was
dying. Would Jesus save him? Christ started for the
house, but when the centurion heard of this he sent a man
to say, "Lord, I am not worthy that you should come under my roof; just say the word and my servant will be
healed." Jesus marveled at the centurion's faith and humility, and when the messenger returned to the house he
found the centurion rejoicing, for the servant was in good
health.

Jesus was especially patient and kind with sinners
who asked for forgiveness. He is the same with us. He

does not turn away from us, even when we disregard him. He is not resentful of our obstinancy. He simply continues to knock at the door of our hearts. And when at long last we open the door, he does not rebuke us, but he comes in and visits with us, friend to friend. To one crowd he told the story of two men who went up to the Temple to pray. The one, a Pharisee, went up to the front and stood there telling God how good he was. He did not pray; he recited a long litany of his virtues. The Pharisee said, "O God, I thank you that I am not like the rest of men, robbers, dishonest, adulterers, or even like that sinner standing there in the back. I fast and I tithe and I do all good things."

The other man told the Lord he was a sinner. In fact, that was about all he said. Over and over, striking his breast, he begged, "O God, be merciful to me, a sinner!"

Jesus concluded, "I tell you this man went back to his house justified rather than the other, for everyone who exalts himself shall be humbled, and he who humbles himself shall be exalted."

With what authority Christ spoke. And with what spiritual insight. Even without his miracles, his words were so sublime that we would know he was from heaven.

(Recite one of the June prayers.)

Reflection for June 22

Jesus told the story of two sons. The father asked them both to go out and work on the farm. The first said, "Yes," but did not go; the second said, "No," but later went. Which best served his father?

He told the tale of the talents, which shows us that

God wants us to use the gifts that He has given us. Indeed that is the best way to express our gratitude. One man was given ten talents, another five, and a third, one. The king left. When he came back he asked for an accounting. The first two had doubled their gifts, and the king said, "Well done, good and faithful servants," and he rewarded them greatly. The man with the one talent had buried his silver piece in the ground. When he told the king this, the monarch was very angry.

And there was the story of the servant who owed his master a great deal of money. The master was going to throw him into prison, but the servant begged for mercy and the debt was forgiven. Then the servant went out and saw a second servant who owed him a small amount. He threatened the second man, who begged for more time, but this was refused and he was thrown into jail.

The master heard of this, however, and he called in the first servant and punished him severely. The point, of course, is that God forgives us many times over and we must forgive our fellow man.

One of his most beautiful parables was that of the Good Samaritan. The hero of the story was a Samaritan, and Jesus was talking to Jews. The Samaritans and Jews got along then about like the Arabs and the Jews today. In the parable a man is attacked by robbers, beaten up, and left for dead. A Jewish priest and then a Levite come along and pass by. Finally, a Samaritan sees the victim and goes down into the ditch to rescue the half-dead Jew.

Jesus told this story in response to a lawyer who asked him, "Who is my neighbor?"

(Recite one of the June prayers.)

Reflection for June 23

Jesus was invited to the home of Mary and Martha, two sisters. When he went in, Martha continued to busy herself about the supper, but Mary sat down at his feet and listened to his wonderful words.

Martha became angry and said to Jesus, "Doesn't it concern you that I am doing all the work?"

Jesus smiled and responded, "Martha, Martha, you are busy about many things, but only one thing counts." He implied that he didn't care what was fixed for supper, or if they ate at all. Mary had chosen the better part.

The most famous parable Jesus told is called "The Prodigal Son." The title, however, is a misnomer. It should be "The Prodigal Father," for the father is the hero of the story, and he is gracious and generous to a fault. And we must remember that the father in this parable is God.

The youth in the story is actually a fool. Like most teens, he thought he was much smarter than his father. The father obviously had a sizable fortune, but the son thought he was not making money fast enough. The youth wanted his inheritance now.

No human father, of course, would be so generous as to comply, but this father does. God is far more generous than we are. The kid takes off for some place like Las Vegas to double his money, and naturally he loses everything. Then one day he wakes up without his money; he wakes up without any of his new friends. And he learns something else. He is not smarter than this father at all — he can't even get a job. He ends up slopping the hogs — and what is more, they are eating better than he is.

Some people have to hit bottom to come to their senses. This is what happened to the boy. He said to himself that he was no longer worthy to be his father's son

for he had disgraced him, but even the farmhands back
home were better off than he was. He would return and
beg his father to be a worker on the farm.

In the meantime, the father (who is God) is out looking for his son. This is the way God is. And when he sees
the son coming, the father rushes to him, forgives all,
and has a big party for him.

(Recite one of the June prayers.)

Reflection for June 24

Jesus was going along the dusty road when he met
ten lepers. The custom then, since this terrible disease
was so dreaded, was that those with leprosy had to live in
isolation, and if others approached, they must cry, "Unclean, unclean!" But when Jesus saw them he went up to
them and touched them and told them they were healed.
He instructed them to show themselves to the authorities
in order to reenter society. They were outcasts no longer.
They went off in a hurry, rejoicing. One, however, realiz-
ing how blessed he was, returned to thank Jesus, glorify-
ing God in a loud voice. He was a Samaritan, a foreigner.
Jesus asked, "Were not all made clean; where are the
other nine? Has no one returned to give glory to God except this stranger?"

When we read of this event we all hang our heads.
How lavish God has been in giving gifts to all of us, countless blessings every day, and we are often too busy to
show our appreciation.

Jesus, in talking to the people, told often of the importance of prayer. He related the story of the man who
had a guest come unexpectedly at night. The man had no
food for him and went rushing over to his neighbor's

house to bang on the door. The neighbor said, "Go away, we are all in bed." But the man continued to knock. The neighbor finally got up and gave him the bread he wanted, not because he was a friend, but because he would not stop knocking.

Here we are taught the importance of perseverance in prayer.

Because prayer is essential, the Apostles said, "Lord, teach us to pray." And Jesus responded by giving them the beautiful Lord's Prayer, the Our Father. Let it be noted of this prayer, our Lord's own prayer, that much of it is concerned with giving glory to God. Too many of our homemade prayers are "gimme" prayers — gimme this and gimme that.

All prayers are answered. There is no such thing as an unanswered prayer. And they are always answered in the best way. Sometimes we cannot see how this is done, but God has promised this and we believe it.

(Recite one of the June prayers.)

Reflection for June 25

The best way to learn to pray is by praying. There are many books on this subject, some good, some not so good, but we can learn more about prayer on our knees than any other way. Father Vincent McNabb, O.P., wrote, "The world is bewildered today. I come across some modern books on prayer and I feel depressed. Then I see some poor old person saying the Rosary, and I cheer up."

Jesus was a man of prayer. He shows us that we must not become discouraged and give up. We know that God answers our prayers. Sometimes we do not see the answer, but we must pray and leave all things in His hands. God is wiser than we are, and He uses every prayer for the best. Archbishop Fulton Sheen said, "God doesn't always give us what we want, but He always gives us what we need."

Sometimes the answer does not suit us at the moment, but later we come to see that God answered us in a way that served us best. Too many times we pray for trinkets, but God wants to make us saints. We go around grieving because we did not get the little gadget we wanted, but God is making us big in heart, a far greater gift indeed.

As Jesus walked from village to village, the sick came streaming to him. He was so kind that they did not hesitate to approach him. They knew they were always welcome. He never turned anyone away, even when he was exhausted.

Once he had spent a whole hectic day with the crowd. The people pressed in upon him and were unruly, but he endured all with the sweetest patience. At the end, some mothers who had come late wanted him to bless their children. To the Apostles, enough was enough, and they started to send the women away. But Jesus heard them and he said, "No, allow the little children to come to me, for of such is the kingdom of God." And he took each child in his arms and blessed them all.

(Recite one of the June prayers.)

Reflection for June 26

Jesus' words had power over minds and hearts. His hands had power to cure the sick in body and soul. Everyone found blessedness and peace in his presence. There was suffering everywhere he went, but with a word Jesus removed so much distress. He laid his hands on the ill and the troubled, and he made them whole again.

But people are peculiar, and some would not accept him. They would watch a great miracle and still would not believe. And even though he was to pay the price in pain, to give his life on the cross to save man, some did not care. Some do not care today.

Stubbornly, some would not let in the light. They preferred the darkness. As St. John wrote, "The light shines in darkness, but the darkness did not comprehend it."

But Jesus continued to preach. He said, "I am the good shepherd. The good shepherd lays down his life for his sheep. The hireling, who is not the shepherd, whose own the sheep are not, sees the wolf coming and runs away, and the wolf snatches the sheep and scatters them. For the hireling has no concern for the flock.

"I am the good shepherd," Jesus repeated, "and I know mine and mine know me. I lay down my life for my sheep. And other sheep I have that are not of this fold. Them also I must bring, and they shall hear my voice, and there shall be one fold and one shepherd."

Many people of good will believed, but others still resisted. They said, "He has a devil; he is mad." But the believers replied, "These are not the words of the devil. Can the devil open the eyes of the blind?"

Jesus told them the story of the man who had a hundred sheep and one of them strayed away. He left the ninety-nine and went out in search of the one that was lost. And when he found it, he rejoiced greatly. Jesus said, "So it is not the will of your Father in heaven that a single one of his little ones shall perish."

(Recite one of the June prayers.)

Reflection for June 27

"Master, how often should a person forgive his neighbor, seven times?" Peter asked. But Christ replied, "Not seven times but seventy times seven times."

All the while the Pharisees were plotting against him. He knew it, but he calmly continued to preach and teach the people. The Pharisees thought, "How can this obscure, unschooled workingman with his ill-smelling fishermen companions tell the people what to do, and worse, try to tell us what to do?"

Jesus said, "I praise You, Father, Lord of heaven and earth, because You have hidden these things from the wise of this world and have let them be known by Your little ones."

With typical courage, Christ went on from village to village telling of the good news that he had brought to earth. His bravery was matched only by his kindness and gentleness. By now the Pharisees, failing to make him look ridiculous with trick questions, were determined to get rid of him one way or another.

He could not stop preaching, for this was his mission. The Father had sent him to bring light and hope to the people, especially the poor and downtrodden, whom he loved in a special way. The will of the Father was his will. And all those who accepted Jesus were loved by the Father. He said, "If a man loves me he will keep my word, and my Father will love him, and we will come to him and make our abode with him."

Jesus drew his strength from the Father; he could comfort the people, so many of them wretched and miserable, because of his closeness to God. He was ever in the presence of the Father, so much so that he could say, "He who sees me sees the Father."

Jesus said, "Peace is my gift to you. The peace that I

will give, the world cannot give. Do not let your hearts be troubled or afraid.''

(Recite one of the June prayers.)

Reflection for June 28

Jesus was preaching in a desert place on the other side of the Sea of Galilee, and a large number of people came out to hear him. They had listened to him for a long time and were hungry. To feed them, he worked a great miracle — the multiplication of the loaves. In so doing, he showed he had power over physical substances like bread. With five barley loaves and two fish, he fed about five thousand.

The huge crowd was so excited that they wanted then and there to take him by force and make him their king. But his kingdom was not of this world, so he slipped away and went up on the mountainside to pray alone.

His disciples got into the boat. It was evening, and they started back across the lake to Capernaum. During the night a storm blew up with a strong wind and high waves. Suddenly they saw Jesus, walking across the water. They were frightened. He said, "It is I; do not be afraid," and he joined them in the boat. In this second great miracle, he showed that he had power over the laws of nature as well as his own body.

The next day he promised the Eucharist, which has to do with bread, his body, and the laws of nature. The crowd had come to him again, curious about how he had crossed the lake, since he had not left in the boat with the Apostles.

Jesus said to them, "You seek me, not to hear my words, but to get more food. I tell you that you should labor for the food that does not perish, but which endures to life everlasting, which the Son of Man will give you."

The crowd said, "Lord, give us this bread always." For he told them the bread that he would give would be the bread from heaven.

Jesus said, "I am the bread of life. . . . I have come down from heaven. . . ."

At this they murmured. How could he say this? "Is this not Jesus, the son of Joseph, whose father and mother we know?" they asked.

But Jesus said again, "I am the bread of life."

(Recite one of the June prayers.)

Reflection for June 29

Jesus said, "I am the bread of life." And he added, "This is the bread that comes down from heaven, so that if anyone eats of this bread he will never die but will live forever. The bread that I will give is my flesh for the life of the world."

The crowd was confused. They murmured, "How can he give us his flesh to eat?"

Jesus answered, "Unless you eat the flesh of the Son of Man and drink his blood, you shall not have life in you. He who eats my flesh and drinks my blood has life everlasting, and I will raise him up on the last day. This is the bread that has come down from heaven; not as your fathers ate manna in the desert and died. He who eats this bread shall live forever."

Many now complained "This is a hard saying, and who can listen to it?" So they departed, and they didn't follow him anymore.

But Jesus looked to the Twelve and said, "Will you

also go away?'' He was willing to lose everyone before he would change one word of his teaching.

Simon Peter answered, "Lord, to whom shall we go? You have the words of everlasting life. We have come to believe and to know that you are the Christ, the Son of God."

These are words we should often repeat.

In promising this, his greatest gift, the Eucharist, Jesus offered hope for the aching hearts of the people. He gave them inspiration and life, a release from their slave-like existence and backbreaking work. The poor people listened and could hardly believe their ears; they hesitated and trembled and wondered if this great good news could possibly be true.

With the Eucharist, Jesus gave courage and light to the people, to their dull, gray lives. And to ours.

(Recite one of the June prayers.)

Reflection for June 30

Jesus continued to mingle with the people, rubbing elbows with them, telling them of the greatness and glory and love of God. He walked the dusty roads from town to town, preaching, healing, seeking sinners. His heart went out to them. They did not fear him as they did the stern and solemn-faced Pharisees. He gave sinners encouragement and comfort such as they had never known before.

We are all sinners, and Jesus seeks each one of us out. In the *Imitation of Christ*, Jesus says, "When you think you are far from me, often it is then that I am closest to you."

We poor stray sheep never seek to return to him as

earnestly as he seeks to find us. He encourages us to acts of penance and prayer and deeds of charity.

He said to his followers, "If any man would be first, he should be last and minister to all." In other words, we are to imitate him. He chastised the Apostles for their childishness in being anxious about position and power. But it did little good. Their baffled faces showed only that their slow minds could not grasp such profound words.

The love that drove Christ to die for us made him reach out to everyone in need. He cast his mercy over the dark lives of the distressed. He was on fire with love for God and his fellow man. When he preached about God, his voice was like thunder and his dark eyes flashed.

Wherever he was, he brought peace to hearts, banishing troubles from worried minds and sin from weak souls.

Jesus constantly preached of love, and it was as if a spring of sweet water suddenly appeared in the desert. And his gentle deeds of kindness continually confirmed his words.

(Recite one of the June prayers.)

Prayers for June

O Sacred Heart of Jesus, living and life-giving fountain of eternal life, infinite treasure of divinity, glowing furnace of love, you are my refuge and my sanctuary. O my adorable and loving Savior, consume my heart with the burning fire of your love; pour down upon my soul the many graces which flow from your Divine Heart, and let my heart be united with yours so that my will may conform to your will. Let all my desires and actions be ruled by your Sacred Heart. Amen.

— St. Gertrude

O admirable Heart of Jesus, heart created expressly for the love of men, pardon me for my sins; help me overcome my ingratitude. O my Jesus, Heart of my Jesus, abyss of love and mercy, you gave your life on the cross for me and you come to me daily in Holy Communion. O Jesus, wound my heart with contrition for my sins and a lively love for you. Through your tears and bloodshed, give me the grace of perseverance in your fervent love until I breathe my last sigh. Amen.

— St. Alphonsus Liguori

O most sweet Jesus, redeemer of the human race, look down upon me, your servant. I am yours and yours I wish to be. And so I consecrate myself to your most Sacred Heart. Have mercy on all men, most merciful Jesus; bless all sinners and bless the poor souls in purgatory. Grant that those who have abandoned you may return to their Father's house lest evil overcome

49

them. Call back all the wayward to your safe harbor of love and truth. Bring peace to the world and blessings to your Church, so that all will with one voice cry out, "Praise be to the divine Heart that purchased our salvation; to it be glory and honor forever." Amen.

Dearest Jesus, with overflowing charity for all, forgive our forgetfulness and our sinfulness. We look to your loving Heart. Please pardon us. Lead us on the path to salvation, O good Shepherd. We implore your assistance, O divine Love. Help us and our loved ones; only with the grace that you give us can we grow in love. O loving Jesus, aid us so that we may persevere in prayer and be faithful to you to the end, so that one day we may come to that happy home where you with the Father and the Holy Spirit live and reign forever and ever. Amen.

O most holy Heart of Jesus, I praise you and thank you for your goodness. I am grateful for the many graces you have given me and my loved ones. I thank you with all my heart; I am deeply appreciative of your gracious generosity. You bless me a thousand times every day, and you shower your graces upon my family and friends. Thank you. May I continue to serve you. May I receive you in Holy Communion with ever greater love. O generous Heart of Jesus, O zealous lover of souls, help me to pray and do penance to my dying day. Give me, please, your grace in abundance; help me to cherish you with all my heart always. Amen.

Sacred Heart of Jesus, who manifested to St. Margaret Mary the desire of reigning in Christian families, we honor you and beg you to bless our home and our family. Grant that your love may be ever in our home. Let there be peace and kindness in our family, and banish sin and evil far from us. Lord Jesus, reign in our minds, give us a simple faith; rule over our hearts so that we may grow in goodness.

O generous Heart of Jesus, bless what we do, our work and our recreation, sanctify our joy, be with us especially in trouble and sickness. You are good and merciful, O adorable Heart of Christ. Be merciful to us, parents and children, and all we love. When we are in sorrow, especially then be beside us. Console us, comfort us, give us strength. And through the intercession of Mary, your Mother and our Mother also, and of good St. Joseph, grant us the love and peace of your Holy Family at Nazareth.

Let us, Heart of Jesus, lover of souls, all be reunited in heaven so that with one another and with you we may be happy forever and ever. Amen.

O Sacred Heart of Jesus, full of compassion, awaiting and welcoming all who pray to you, please help me. Your love for us cannot be put in human words. I praise you, dearest Lord; I thank you for the many graces you have given me and my loved ones. You have bestowed upon us so many wonderful blessings. Humbly I express my appreciation. Thank you in particular for the great gifts of the Mass and the Blessed Sacrament, and for giving us your loving Mother Mary to be our advocate. Protect my home and family, my relatives and friends. Assist all those in need, especially all who need you the most. My Jesus, I love you with my whole heart. I grieve for having offended you. Forgive me. Though I am unworthy, I pledge myself to you, O Sacred Heart of Jesus. I desire most of all your holy love and my final perseverance. I unite myself to your most loving Heart, and I beseech the Father to accept my prayers for love of you. Amen.

Jesus, our Savior, O Sacred Heart, I pray to you and ask you, O Heart full of love, to take care of my family, the sick, those who are dying today, and all in need. Help all poor sinners. Bless the poor souls in purgatory. Give your special assistance to the hungry and to the people who live as slaves under dictators. Jesus, you are the source of every good. You said, "If anyone thirsts let him come to me." I come to you now and beg your help. I love you, praise you, give you thanks, and ask for your aid. I am poor, and you are rich; I am sick, and you are the physician of souls; I thirst, and you are the fountain of life and goodness. Most amiable, sweet, beloved Jesus, please hear my prayers. Amen.

O Christ Jesus, whose pierced Heart is the fountain of all graces, the wellspring of our many blessings, we are grateful for your mercy and forgiveness and for your unchanging message of love. In your generous kindness help us, make us grow in faith and goodness.

You have in so many ways blessed our family. We thank you with all our hearts. We can but look to you to inspire us and to continue to help us as we journey on our way to heaven. Amen.

O good Jesus, we look at the cross and see how you love us. You gave your life to save us from sin and to gain heaven for us. You suffered so very much; your Sacred Heart was broken, all because you wished to help us. You loved us even unto death. We go to your Heart, burning with love, and beg your gracious blessings. Amen.

Most loving Jesus, my Lord and my God, my hope and helper, thank you for the graces you have given me. Help me to serve you better and to do what I can to make others love you more. I confide my salvation to your care. Accept me for your servant, deliver me from temptations, and please give me the strength to triumph over evil until death. With you at my side I hope to die a good death. You love me, and I beseech you to assist me at all times with your love, but especially at the last moment of my life. Leave me not, until you see me safe in heaven, blessing you and singing your mercies for all eternity. So I hope; so may it be. Amen.

Lord Jesus, the love of my soul, you desire so much to be loved by us. Come, then, and take possession of my heart, so that I may be more like your Sacred Heart. This is my ardent desire. Dear Redeemer, be with me, for you are my delight. Let me treasure your love. Make me forget myself and only remember your goodness. Teach me to love you more and more, and to please you in what I do. Guard me and guide me always. My Jesus, I embrace you and unite myself to you. I beg your pardon for my sins and fervently ask that I may spend my eternity in your loving heavenly home. Amen.

Thank you, dear Jesus, for protecting us and keeping us safe. Please continue to show us your mercy. We beseech you, O Sacred Heart, lover of all mankind, in your great goodness, to bless us all the day long and keep us through the night. Grant that we may live each day with you and for you. Free us from anger and fear and aid us in overcoming all temptations. May we work and do all things for love of you. You became man to free us from sin and to gain heaven for us. We are most grateful. Amen.

Jesus, Lord of mercies, O Sacred Heart full of comfort, send your blessings upon us. May we use your graces well. We pray and beseech your goodness, O lover of men; be mindful of our daily needs, for we can do nothing without you. Bless all your faithful people, dear Lord, and bless all poor sinners. O Christ Jesus, Son of God, listen to our plea. All your children on earth are in need. Our hearts yearn for your assistance. You know how much we need you. Hear us, Lord, hear us. Amen.

I speak to you, dear Jesus, though I am a sinner. I come to you because you said that I should. I cannot pray well, but I know you understand. You were so kind and understanding to sinners when you walked in the world. I take courage from reading in the Gospel of your goodness. Teach me to pray; help me to be more humble. Forgive me, Jesus. Let your kind mercy wash over me and cleanse me. There is no confidence except in your mercy. Save me. Let your love and your truth fill my heart. Amen.

O my Lord, you are such a great comfort to me. Grant me your grace, most merciful Jesus. Be with me, work with me and stay with me, Lord, to the end. May I desire to do your will. But I cannot do this alone; if you do not help me, I will fail. May your name be ever glorified. I give you my love. Amen.

O kind Lord Jesus, may joy and peace be with us, may your grace and comfort and love fill our hearts. Strengthen us so that we may do your holy will and faithfully persevere to the end. Come to us, embrace us, bless us. You are the truth and the life. There is no other. There is no happiness without you. You are the very source of pity; have pity on us. Do not turn away from us, for we need you desperately. We put all our hope in your countless mercies. Amen.

Please look down with kindness, Jesus, upon the sick. With your healing power help them. Help the poor, the afflicted, and the abandoned. Soothe them in their sorrow and pain. Be their saving remedy. Bless all in trials and dangers, we humbly beseech you. Keep them close to your Sacred Heart. Give strength to their weakness, raise up their spirits, console and comfort them. Amen.

O best and truest Friend, dear Jesus, give comfort to those in sorrow and especially to those who have lost a loved one so dear to their hearts. Death is a part of life; please help the grieving to see that it is but a door through which we pass from this world into the glory of eternal life. Be merciful, Lord; we call upon the special blessings of your loving Sacred Heart to give your grace to the sorrowing family and ease their suffering. Amen.

O Jesus, my light and my sanctification, fill my soul with your grace and grant that I may grow in faith. I praise you and love you; may I do so even more. I am unworthy, dear Lord. I am sorry for my sins. Forgive me, I beg you. May your holy Mother help me. O Sacred Heart of Jesus, heal my soul with your love. My love is weak; strengthen me. Let my soul hasten to your embrace; shelter me in your Sacred Heart. I can do no good if you are not with me. You have blessed me so wonderfully in the past, you have been so good and gracious to my family and loved ones; bless us this day and always. Amen.

Jesus Lord, you are my hope and the joy of my heart. Help me to love you more and more. Without you I am nothing and I can do nothing. Look, I beseech you, upon my family and bless them with your graces. Save us and help us, O Lord. Draw us closer, O Christ, to your Sacred Heart. Hold us and heal us. Take away our hostility and fill our hearts with your gracious and generous love. Let your goodness flow over us. Cast out fear, renew our faith, take away anxiety, give us your peace. May our family grow in kindness for love of you. Amen.

Give your special blessings this day to those who are suffering trials; in particular, look with kindness upon the anxious and the oppressed and those who are ill. Save all poor sinners. Heal, protect, and strengthen all of those in need. Comfort them with the comfort of your Sacred Heart, dear Christ. Amen.

Direct us, O Jesus, in your ways. You are the way, the truth, and the life. Lead us along the path of goodness. You are the source of all knowledge: show us the road to wisdom. Bless us with humility, which is the beginning of wisdom. Give us your heavenly insights so that we can help others along the way. Without you all knowledge is vain. Pour your love into our souls, dearest Lord. Amen.

Lord Jesus, be my peace of soul. Let me live serenely in your love. Do not let me give way to anxiety and anguish, but embolden me to put all things in your hands and not worry.

Lord Jesus, in your mercy, be with me always. You are my closest Friend, O Christ. Help me to live a good life. Let the love of your Sacred Heart show through me. May I give your kindness to my neighbors. Confirm and strengthen me, O Lord, so that I will grow in grace and graciousness and generosity. Amen.

Litany of the Sacred Heart of Jesus

Lord, have mercy on us.

Christ, have mercy on us.

Lord, have mercy on us.

Christ, hear us.

Christ, graciously hear us.

God, the Father of Heaven, *have mercy on us.**

God, the Son, Redeemer of the world,*

God the Holy Spirit,

Holy Trinity, one God,

Heart of Jesus, Son of the eternal Father,

Heart of Jesus, formed by the Holy Spirit in the womb of the Virgin Mother,

Heart of Jesus, substantially united to the Word of God,

Heart of Jesus, of infinite majesty,

Heart of Jesus, holy temple of God,

Heart of Jesus, tabernacle of the most High,

Heart of Jesus, house of God and gate of heaven,

Heart of Jesus, burning furnace of divine love,

Heart of Jesus, abode of justice and love,

Heart of Jesus, full of kindness and love,

Heart of Jesus, abyss of all virtues,

Heart of Jesus, most worthy of all praise,

Heart of Jesus, king and center of all hearts,

Heart of Jesus, in which are all treasures of wisdom and knowledge,

Heart of Jesus, in whom dwells the fullness of the Divinity,

Heart of Jesus, in which the Father is well pleased,

Heart of Jesus, of whose fullness we have all received,

Heart of Jesus, desire of the everlasting hills,

Heart of Jesus, patient and most merciful,

Have mercy on us is repeated after each invocation.

Heart of Jesus, rich to all who call upon you,
Heart of Jesus, fountain of life and holiness,
Heart of Jesus, propitiation for our sins,
Heart of Jesus, burdened with opprobrium,
Heart of Jesus, bruised for our offenses,
Heart of Jesus, obedient unto death,
Heart of Jesus, pierced with a lance,
Heart of Jesus, source of all consolation,
Heart of Jesus, our life and resurrection,
Heart of Jesus, our peace and reconciliation,
Heart of Jesus, victim for our sins,
Heart of Jesus, salvation of those who hope in you,
Heart of Jesus, hope of those who die in you,
Heart of Jesus, delight of all the saints,
Lamb of God, who take away the sins of the world, spare
    us, O Lord.
Lamb of God, who take away the sins of the world,
    graciously hear us, O Lord.
Lamb of God, who take away the sins of the world, have
    mercy on us.

V. Jesus, meek and humble of Heart,

R. Make our hearts like unto yours.

Let Us Pray

O Almighty and eternal God, look down upon the
Heart of your most beloved Son and upon the praises and
satisfactions which he offers to you on behalf of all sinners, and do you, appeased by these appeals to your
mercy, grant us pardon, in the name of Jesus Christ,
your Son, who lives and reigns with you, world without
end. Amen.

PROMISES TO ST. MARGARET MARY
(For those devoted to the Sacred Heart)

1. I will give them all the graces necessary for their state in life.

2. I will establish peace in their families.

3. I will console them in their difficulties.

4. I will be their secure refuge during life and more especially at the hour of death.

5. I will shower down abundant blessings on all their undertakings.

6. Sinners shall find in my Heart a source and boundless ocean of mercy.

7. Tepid souls shall become fervent.

8. Fervent souls shall rise speedily to great perfection.

9. I will bless the houses in which the picture of my Sacred Heart shall be placed and honored.

10. I will give priests the power of touching the most hardened heart.

11. Persons who spread this devotion shall have their names written in my Heart, and they shall never be effaced therefrom.

12. I will grant the grace of final repentance to all those who shall receive Holy Communion on the first Friday for nine months consecutively. My divine Heart will become their refuge in their last moments.

II. JULY: Month of the Precious Blood

O Jesus, whose precious blood

was shed for me,

have mercy on us.

During July, through these daily readings and prayers, we reflect on the wondrous truth that Jesus gave his life for us.

July Devotions

Reflection for July 1

They were crossing the lake, but Jesus was weary and fell asleep on a cushion in the stern of the boat. A squall came up, and the fierce, sudden wind and waves were beating against the small vessel. The Apostles were frightened. They rushed to Jesus and woke him up, shouting above the wind, "Master, don't you care? We are going to perish!"

Jesus stood up and rebuked the wind and said to the sea, "Peace. Be still!" And calm came over the lake. He turned to his companions and said, "Why are you fearful, O you of little faith?"

They were amazed. In awe they said, "What manner of man is this, that even the wind and the sea obey him?"

Not only was what he did extraordinary, so also were his words. "Be simple as children," he said. "Heaven and earth shall pass away but my word shall not pass away," he stated. And he said, "The grain of wheat . . . if it dies, then it yields rich fruit."

Jesus said, "Be wise as serpents and as simple as doves." He told them, "He who follows me can never walk in darkness; he will possess the light which is life." He added, "I will show you the way." In speaking of good deeds he related, "As long as you did it for the least of my little ones, you did it for me." He said, "What does it profit a man to gain the whole world and lose his own immortal soul?"

How different he was from the other religious leaders and teachers. The goodness of his soul shone through his brilliant eyes. His face reflected heaven. One look at him often transformed souls.

Jesus could have been rich, but he chose to be poor; he was a person of strength, but also of mildness. As François Mauriac wrote, "How magnificent is faith in a God who is our brother."

We know so little about life and death, and so we turn to Jesus. He is our guide. We need nothing more.

(Recite one of the July prayers beginning on page 99.)

Reflection for July 2

We grow weary in life. It is Jesus who rescues us. As the undecipherable riddle of life confronts us, we look to our Lord. We do not know God; we do not even know ourselves. We ourselves are a mystery to us. We can only turn to Jesus. All we know really is what he told us. And he told us all we really need to know, and that is that God is Love.

The poverty of Jesus mocked the wealth of the mighty. His humility showed up the small-minded pride of the self-centered.

Christ told the crowd marvelous things: we are made in the image and likeness of God; it is by sin that we deface the likeness. It is the disorder of sin that brings ugliness into the world. Vanity, sloth, dishonesty, cowardice, snobbishness, and sensuality makes humans less than human.

When the evil sap is stealing upward, a poison permeates our system. Then, we must cry out to the Savior, as did Peter when sinking in the sea, "Lord, save me, I am perishing." We must pray, "Lamb of God, you who take away the sins of the world, have mercy on us."

Jesus is our dearest Friend. To help us he came and "pitched his tent among us." He came "that we may have life and have it to the fullest." Because he was human, he knows our happiness and heartbreak.

Jesus was sent, in the words of Michael Novak, as "a freely given intention of God's love." God, as it were, disguised himself in a humble human form to civilize us and lead us to the triumph of love. Jesus came to us to soften the hostile influence of the warrior barbarian in our hearts. The conflict between love and hatred, this civil war within us, goes on daily; it is a constant, continuous struggle. We cannot be victorious without Christ.

We look around in the world, we read the newspapers, and there is so much evil, suffering, and pain. We must pray over and over, "Come, Lord Jesus."

(Recite one of the July prayers.)

Reflection for July 3

The brother of Martha and Mary, Jesus' friend Lazarus, was very sick. When Jesus heard this, however, he said simply, "This sickness is not unto death, but for the glory of God, that through it the Son of God may be glorified," and he went on about his teaching.

Later he commented, "Lazarus, our friend, sleeps." Still later he said, "Let us now go to him."

When he arrived in Bethany, where his friends lived, Lazarus had been buried four days. Martha heard that Jesus had arrived and she went out to him. She said, "Lord, if you had been here my brother would not have died. But even now I know that whatever you shall ask God, He will give it to you."

Jesus said, "Your brother will rise from the dead." Martha in tears replied, "I know that he will do so at the resurrection on the last day." But Jesus said, "I am the resurrection and the life; he who believes in me, even if he dies, shall live, and whoever lives and believes in me shall never die. Do you believe this?"

Martha said, "Yes, Lord, I believe that you are the Christ, the Son of God, who has come into the world."

She then went and called her sister Mary to come. When Mary left the house the people said she was going to the tomb of her brother, and they followed her.

Jesus was at the tomb, and he wept for his friend. The crowd whispered, "Could not he who opened the eyes of the blind have caused this man not to die?"

Jesus said, "Take away the stone from the tomb." But Mary replied that her brother had been buried already for four days and was decaying.

However, Jesus said, "Father, I give you thanks that you have heard me." Then he cried, "Lazarus, come forth!" And at once, he who had been dead came forth, bound hands and feet with the burial bandages.

(Recite one of the July prayers.)

Reflection for July 4

Jesus is our strength. Despite our foolishness, sin, and selfishness, he loves us with all his heart. Though at times we feel we are drowning in our mediocrity and shallowness, Christ assists us. He came to shatter the "sorrowful, weary wheel of existence."

Jesus was loved because he loved. He preached with loving intensity. But in his deeds, he was even more loving. On one occasion he was in Jerusalem. The Pharisees brought him a woman caught in adultery. According to Jewish law, she should be stoned to death. Trying to involve him, they threw her at his feet and said, "What do you say?"

Jesus did not answer. Instead he stooped down and began writing with a stick in the sand. He then stood up and said, "Let him who is without sin cast the first stone." They were befuddled, for looking at his writing in the sand, they may have imagined they saw their sins.

Again he stooped down and began to write. This time, when he stood up, no one was there. All the bold accusers had silently slipped away; they were apparently scared to death that he would write their names behind their sins.

Jesus, looking around, said to the woman, "Is there no one here to condemn you?"

Tearfully she whispered, "No one, Lord." Seconds before, she had been sure that she was going to be stoned to death. She was still sobbing and trembling.

Jesus said, "Then neither will I condemn you. Go in peace and sin no more."

She could not believe it. Dragged here to be killed, she was suddenly free. She could only kiss his sacred hand and rush away.

(Recite one of the July prayers.)

Reflection for July 5

Jesus lived in Palestine, a land of no great importance. He was born in a cave and grew up in the remote village of Nazareth, which even the people of Palestine looked down upon. "Can anything good come out of Nazareth?" Nathaniel asked.

In truth, if Jesus were looking for success in the eyes of the world, he went about it all wrong: he preached to the poor and did not even try to impress the important people. He spoke out directly and honestly, telling the Pharisees just what they were — a terrible mistake if he wanted political prestige. Indeed, because he spoke out even when it was unpopular, it cost him his life.

Jesus made the comfortable uncomfortable, telling the truth rather than using slogans and catchwords to capture the crowd.

People in his day, and in our own, have told us we must reform the world. Jesus told us we must reform ourselves. We will make the world better when we make ourselves better. Most reformers want to reform everyone else except themselves. Purge your own heart of hostility: that is the first step, Jesus told us.

Most experts would rather be fashionable than right. Jesus contended that one must not cater to the times. He opposed the ways of the world, which in the end always fail a person, as the Lord tells us. In the words of Francis Thompson, "All things betray thee, who betrayest Me."

Jesus was unique. He seemed in truth from another world. The people were held fast by his words; a force radiated from him that gripped them. Unlike that of the Pharisees, his speech was not cold and rigid, but warm and profound, with power and energy. He called everyone to greatness. In his presence there was a sense of the divine.

(Recite one of the July prayers.)

Reflection for July 6

Jesus was passing by, and he saw a man blind from birth. His disciples asked, "Master, who has sinned, this man or his parents, that he should be born blind?" It was the thinking at that time that if a person was handicapped he was being punished for his sins — just the opposite of the teaching of Jesus, who tells us that those who suffer are his special friends. And so he explained to his followers that day that suffering is not a punishment but a challenge for people to grow in soul. And he cured the man.

The people said, "Is this not he who used to sit and beg?" Some replied, "Yes," but others did not agree. The man, however, said, "I am he." So they asked, "How then were your eyes opened?" He answered," The man called Jesus cured me."

His neighbors took the man to the Pharisees. They were angry because Jesus had cured him on the Sabbath, when no one was supposed to work. The Pharisees said of Jesus, "This man is not from God, for he does not keep the Sabbath." To them their petty little laws were what was important, not the great miracle.

Jesus had argued this point before, calling the Pharisees hypocrites. He said if they had an animal that fell in a ditch, they would at once get him out, Sabbath or no Sabbath. Now they were condemning him for doing a kind deed on this day. The people did not agree with the Pharisees; they said, "But how can a man who is a sinner work these great signs?" And this made the religious leaders all the more angry.

The Pharisees asked the man, "What do you say of him who opened your eyes?" He replied, "He is a prophet." The leaders were irate at such a true answer. They decided that the man must not have been blind at all.

They asked his parents, "Is this your son, of whom you say that he was born blind? How then does he now see?" The parents were fearful, for the Pharisees said they would expel anyone who followed Jesus from the synagogue. They were evasive, saying that they knew he was born blind, but they did not know how he now saw. "Ask him; he is old enough to answer for himself."

(Recite one of the July prayers.)

Reflection for July 7

The man born blind who was cured by Jesus was summoned again by the Pharisees. The leaders said they knew that Jesus was a sinner. But, much to their consternation, the other said, "Whether he is a sinner or not, I do not know. One thing I do know, that whereas I was blind, now I see." He continued, "Why do you question me again? Do you also wish to become his disciples?"

At this the Pharisees almost had apoplexy. They shouted loudly, "You may be his disciple, but we are disciples of Moses. We know that God spoke to Moses, but as for this man, we do not know where he is from."

The man who was cured said, "It is marvelous. He opened my eyes. We know that God does not hear sinners, yet this man did this for me. If anyone worships God and does His will, God hears him. Not from the beginning of the world has it been known that anyone opened the eyes of a man born blind. If this man was not from God, he could not do this."

In his simple way he was telling the Pharisees that they should open their eyes. They cried out, "You, who were born blind and therefore are a sinner, presume to teach us?"

Later, when Jesus heard of these things he sought out the man and said to him, "Do you believe in the Son of God?"

"Who is he, Lord, that I may believe in him?"

Jesus said, "You have seen him, and it is he who is speaking with you."

The man fell down with his face to the ground and said, "I believe, Master."

Many others however would not believe. "He came unto his own and his own received him not."

(Recite one of the July prayers.)

Reflection for July 8

Christ chose a very commonplace group to be his disciples. Anybody who was anybody would not associate with them, and certainly not the great and the powerful. But the Apostles were gradually learning. They had the key to all friendship with God; they were good of heart.

The Pharisees, on the other hand, were outraged at everything Jesus said. They said he was a seducer and must be silenced. What they meant was that he was too personable and winning in his ways and the people loved him. He therefore must be removed from the scene. His powerful preaching, his magnetic personality must be stopped so the people would return to the Pharisees and their dull, humdrum words. Jesus was ruining the people, they said, but it was really his forceful, forthright accusations that bitterly stung these pompous teachers.

In the end they would defeat Christ by nailing him to the cross. In perpetrating this wretched murder, they would think they had won, and on Good Friday their spirits would soar. But as we know, God snatched victory from defeat; in fact, Jesus won out by means of his failure. As he said after the Resurrection, "Was it not expected that the Christ should undergo these sufferings and so enter into his glory?"

Jerusalem was now his destiny. Jesus knew his days were numbered. He must suffer the ordeal for which he was sent; he must fulfill his mission, to endure the passion and to die, to be the Savior of mankind.

He now left Galilee and set his feet on the road to the great capital city where all this would happen. As he walked along, never having felt so alone, he could close his eyes and see the black cross of Calvary silhouetted against the bleak sky.

(Recite one of the July prayers.)

Reflection for July 9

More than once Jesus had told the Apostles about his final days, the destiny that awaited him. He would go up to Jerusalem, where he would suffer and be put to death, but he would rise again. The Apostles were always depressed by such terrible words of gloom. They did not want him to go, but he insisted, for according to the divine plan he had a rendezvous with death. The little bewildered band walked behind him, afraid and dismayed. What kind of madness was this?

When Jesus arrived at Jerusalem, the common people were so happy to see him coming again that they spontaneously formed a joyful procession and wildly cheered him. They pulled branches from the palm trees and waved them in the air, shouting, "Hosanna to the son of David! Blessed is he who comes in the name of the Lord!"

This made the Pharisees even more furious. They were green with jealousy. They knew they had to get rid of him, even if it meant murder. They said it was their patriotic duty, it was for the good of the people, when all the while they meant that their envy was eating them up.

On that first Palm Sunday Jesus went to the Temple and found there the merchants buying and selling. They did this everywhere in Jerusalem, to be sure, but now they had invaded the very House of God. He angrily pushed over the tables and chased them out. He quoted Scripture: "My house is a house of prayer, but you have made it a den of thieves."

To be sure, these men of business went rushing to the Pharisees to protest, adding fuel to the fire.

In the meantime, Matthew tells us, "the blind and the lame came to him in the Temple, and he healed them." But the more wondrous his works, the more indignant the religious leaders became. The showdown was near.

(Recite one of the July prayers.)

Reflection for July 10

Though Jesus knew his life now could be measured in hours, he continued to give himself to the people. He must tell them to his dying breath of the great goodness of God.

Preaching in Jerusalem, despite the looming menace, showed true courage; he continued to teach there at peril of his life. Every day the enemy was plotting vengeance. But he loved the people so much he could not leave them. And the people loved him, for his words were full of the music of mercy.

He told them they must pray often; there are some things that only God can give this poor, bleeding world. It is as though he were talking to us today. Our world is also sick, dehumanized by bigness and machines. God is the only one that really thinks an individual is important. He loves each one so much; he loves you so much that he was willing to give everything, even life itself, for you. He does not ask you to die for him, but he died for you.

Jesus calls us away from the busyness and noise of our mixed-up, weary world. He wishes to make us happy; he alone can do so.

We must pray for divine guidance. All great men always did this; only the small-minded and the small of heart think they do not need Jesus — and end up empty-handed on a dead-end road. No wonder pessimism is the philosophy of our times.

Jesus taught us the meaning of suffering: it is the road to God. He himself accepted suffering; he did not reject pain, he took it upon himself and used it for good. He cast himself into the midst of men in all their distress and sorrow, and with love he shared their cross and carried it on his bloody shoulders.

(Recite one of the July prayers.)

Reflection for July 11

One day Jesus looked down from the terrace of the Temple, down on the houses of Jerusalem huddled together on the narrow winding streets crowded with people, and with sorrow he predicted its destruction. The disciples were shaken by his words and his continual insistence that a catastrophe was to come upon him.

Another day, teaching in the Temple on Solomon's

porch, he saw a widow quietly put a penny in the poor box. Previously a number of wealthy individuals had been dropping in gold pieces with a great deal of fanfare. Jesus said, "Blessed is that woman. What she gives is more important than the large gifts of the rich men. They gave from their surplus, but she is giving from her grocery money."

Then he said something startling. He stated that the ancient patriarch Abraham was "proud to see the day of my coming; he saw it and rejoiced." But the people asked, "Have you seen Abraham? You are not yet fifty years old."

Jesus replied solemnly, "Believe me, before Abraham came to be, I AM." Here he proclaimed his divinity without reservation. The time was drawing short, and he must make all things clear.

On Wednesday the tragic drama of Holy Week picks up the pace. Judas had become disillusioned with the Master. He was one of those who thought that Christ was going to lead a rebellion and throw the Roman conquerors out of their land, but it was now evident that he was not interested in political or military maneuvers.

As far as Judas was concerned, Jesus had squandered his magnificent gifts. Here he could have been a great leader, immortalized in history as a liberator, and all he ever talked about was love, peace and brotherhood.

Judas intended to leave him, as any reasonable man should.

(Recite one of the July prayers.)

Reflection for July 12

Just when Judas was planning to desert that dreamer Jesus, it came to him that perhaps he could make some money out of this. He did love money, and it was inevitable that the Master would one way or another fall into the hands of the Pharisees. They were growing angrier every day. Christ was more popular with the people than ever, and here he was now under their very nose, teaching in the very Temple, which they considered their preserve; after all, they were the authorized teachers of religion.

Judas knew it was impossible not to love Jesus, and yet he was so unrealistic. War, not love, was what solved problems, Judas thought. If you loved the brutish Roman soldiers, their answer was to kick you in the teeth.

Why did Jesus try to teach the multitude in their rags? Why didn't he try to persuade important people like the Pharisees, Judas mused. Oh, to be sure, he would have to flatter the old fools and water down his strong words, but they were the influential individuals. As he thought about it, however, he knew how useless it was to even suggest such a thing to Jesus. He would never change a word, come what may. And the worst was coming. Because Jesus would not change, he was doomed. Because he insisted on giving himself night and day to the poor, bleating sheep that crowded around him, in the end no one would be able to save him.

Indeed Jesus did not just give himself to the dirty, unruly mob, but he spoke of giving himself *for* them; he seemed unable to do otherwise. How did he ever expect to get anywhere if he did not court the upper class? Jesus said that he was the shepherd who guarded his flock. He said, "The good shepherd lays down his life for his sheep." But Judas asked himself, "What good can he do us if he is dead?"

(Recite one of the July prayers.)

Reflection for July 13

The whole adventure with Jesus had seemed so promising to Judas in the beginning, but now, without doubt, it was destined for failure. In fact, Judas thought, Jesus seemed determined on self-destruction. Judas mused, "Since there is no doubt that the whole thing is going to come crashing down, wouldn't it be wise for me to bail out — and make a little money too?"

So he went to the residence of the High Priest next to the Temple and was told he would be given thirty pieces of silver if he would lead the guards to Jesus at night. They did not want to seize him during the day for fear the people would start a riot.

Judas agreed to help them. The very next night, he would take them out to where Jesus was praying.

The next day was the feast of the Passover, the greatest Jewish celebration. All devout people celebrated the day with an evening meal like the final supper the Jews ate in Egypt before Moses led them out of slavery.

Jesus and his Apostles had their Passover meal in the upper room lent to them by a friend. It was, unknown to the Apostles, Jesus' farewell meal, and Christians call it the Last Supper.

Since they were poor and did not have a servant to wash the dust off their feet, Jesus himself, the Master, did this. He said his followers must minister to one another, and here at his last meal with his closest friends he dramatized this teaching for them. Jesus abased himself. Worldly leaders are self-asserting; Christian leaders must be self-abnegating. The Christ-follower must serve, not be served. "The first shall be last" in Christ's kingdom of love.

(Recite one of the July prayers.)

Reflection for July 14

At the Last Supper they began by thanking God for His gifts. They performed the traditional ceremonies and sang the psalm, "Not to us, Lord, not to us be glory; let thy name alone be honored; thine the merciful, thine the faithful. Praise the Lord, for abundant has his mercy been toward us."

During the meal Jesus said, "I tell you in truth, one of you is about to betray me." The Apostles, in confusion and sadness, each said, "Is it I, Lord?" John, next to him, heard him tell, "It is the one to whom I give the dish." And he gave it to Judas. Jesus said, trying to dissuade Judas, "The Son of Man goes his way, it is written of him, but woe to that man by whom the Son of Man is betrayed."

Seeing his warning had no impact, Jesus said to Judas, "What you have to do, do quickly."

The traitor got up and left the lighted room and went out into the darkness, rushing down the stairs into the crooked alley below, heading in haste for the residence of the High Priest.

Jesus then said, "With longing I have longed to eat this meal with you." In truth Jesus at Mass says these words to us each day.

Then, miracle of miracles, he gave to them — and to all of us — the Holy Eucharist, which he had promised, "the bread of heaven." Christ's love for man is never satisfied; his love compelled him by this Blessed Sacrament to enter into an even closer union with our souls. Only a divine mind could have devised this means whereby he could return to the Father and yet remain with us.

When Jesus had previously promised the Eucharist, some could not believe it. Since humans are not very generous, they could not comprehend how God could be so

supremely generous. Their skepticism and cynicism triumphed, and they doubted the Lord. But Jesus did indeed
give himself to us in the Blessed Sacrament. Humans
must never try to measure God's overwhelming love by
the feebleness of man's love.

(Recite one of the July prayers.)

Reflection for July 15

Taking bread at the Last Supper, Jesus said, "This is
my Body. . . ." Taking the chalice of wine, he said, "This
is my Blood. . . ." And he gave it to the others as food for
their souls. He then said, "Do this in memory of me."
His followers are to consecrate as he consecrated, and so
today the renewal of the Last Supper, following his command, is called the Mass. At Mass, in the Holy Sacrament, just as the Apostles did at the Last Supper, we receive Christ into our hearts, we drink of the very fountain
of living water. And we say with St. Paul, "We live in
him and by him. . . . it is Christ who lives in me." The
Body which was given for us is given to us.

We cannot comprehend this tremendous mystery; it
is foolish to try. All we need to know is that in Holy Communion we are most intimately united with Christ our
Lord, and with his life-giving love.

When he walked in the world, Jesus influenced countless people. He exercises an even more profound influence on our souls in Holy Communion. No one can be in
the company of the Lord without being inspired by him.
In the Eucharist we encounter Christ most especially;
we experience a personal meeting with Jesus, who brings
love to us which we can never create. Let us fix our eyes
upon him and be stirred by him, the fountain of all grace.

The Eucharist is the supreme expression of the love of Jesus for us. Christ, after all, can give no more nor better than himself. He seeks to excite us to deeds of kindness so that he can express his love through us.

We poor humans, vessels of clay, need so much help before we can become even a little more Christlike. What we know most of all is that we need Christ more than anything and that we should frequently nourish our souls with the Eucharist. It is our "pledge of future glory." St. Thomas Aquinas said that the Eucharist is our strength to overcome temptations and the source of a sympathetic heart.

(Recite one of the July prayers.)

Reflection for July 16

In the Eucharist Jesus invites us. He says, "Come to me, all you who are weary and overburdened, and I will refresh you." He knows your troubles and worries, your pains and trials. Did he ever in the Gospel let suffering go unrelieved? And the Savior is the same today; he awaits you to help you.

We should beg our Lord to fashion our souls after his own. We should ask him to penetrate our hearts and take possession of us, to expel our egotism and weakness. We should approach him with faith: the greater the faith, the greater the grace.

The Eucharist is the center of the Church and has been so for nearly two thousand years. All the saints had a tremendous devotion to the Blessed Sacrament.

At the Last Supper, after Jesus had given the precious, priceless gift of the Eucharist, after he had given himself to the Apostles, the time had come to leave. In the Blessed Sacrament, Christ tells us, "I have bestowed my love upon you, just as my Father has bestowed His love upon me. Live on in my love." But now the Paschal meal was over; now he must drink the chalice of suffering to the very dregs and fulfill his Father's will not just in words but in deeds.

After they had sung the traditional final hymn in the upper room, they left and went out into the black of the night. Christ and his companions moved through the narrow streets in shadows and out through the city walls to the Mount of Olives, where he frequently prayed.

They passed near the High Priest's residence, and perhaps they noticed some commotion going on there, for Judas had already betrayed the Master and the Pharisees were beginning to assemble the temple guards.

They passed through the gate and crossed the little stream of the Cedron and came to Gethsemani, a grove of olive trees. Jesus asked the Apostles to pray with him, but they fell asleep.

(Recite one of the July prayers.)

Reflection for July 17

In the Garden of Gethsemani, Jesus took the three leaders, Peter, John, and James, with him a little further on, and he said, "Watch and pray with me. My soul is sad, even unto death." He fell to the ground praying, "Father, if it be possible, let this cup pass from me; nevertheless, not my will but Thy will be done." Christ, who had experienced discomfort and poverty, hunger and thirst and pain, now experienced fear and failure and agony. He felt the deep sorrow of desolation and betrayal. St. Paul said, "Him who was without sin God made to be sin for us." All this he endured to expiate our sins. In his life Jesus taught the way of wholeness (holiness); in his passion he taught the value of suffering.

Jesus completely surrendered his will to the Father. Still, fear engulfed him and he said, "My soul is ready to die with sorrow." Father Gerald Vann, O.P., notes: "We live today in a world haunted by fear and anxiety, so the agony of Jesus is very close to us." In truth, these days there is a kind of hopelessness in the air, a certain futility; anguish hangs heavy in the hearts of men.

At Gethsemani, Jesus was afraid just as *we* are. He was tormented with a deep dread; the black waters of near-despair seemed to close in over his head. He cried out in anguish and shed tears of fear, while drops of bloody sweat drenched his trembling body. The thought that mankind, whom he would die to save, seemed determined to drown itself in evil — that thought was like a river of sorrow in his heart. He had spent all those days teaching people about the richness of God's love for them and how tragedy comes when humans reject Him. But many souls would choose sin and self-destruction.

Despite all he did, many would ignore him, many would doubt him, many would curse him and throw in their lot with the Prince of Darkness and his hatred.

(Recite one of the July prayers.)

Reflection for July 18

Jesus went back to the Apostles and found them sleeping. He said, "Can you not watch one hour with me? Watch, and pray, so that you will not enter into temptation."

He says these selfsame words to us. We cannot possibly overcome the many temptations all around us today and we will never be wise in the things of God unless we watch and pray. We must not sleep like the Apostles while the Son of Man suffers.

His slow-witted disciples only turned over and went back to sleep. Even his chosen ones did not support him in his hour of need.

Jesus was alone, all alone. The tragedy of the passion was upon him, and horrible pain swayed his soul. When he thought of the many empty-hearted individuals who would call themselves Christians but would live like barbarians, his Sacred Heart broke in two. He would give his very life, all that he had to give, and many would remain indifferent. The apathy that would be widespread among his future followers appalled him.

There was some comfort. He knew that some, down through the years, would find new heart because of what he taught and what he was doing. But these would be a handful compared to the crowds seemingly bent on sin and strife. Inhuman iniquity in the world was too much to think about, and he became bathed in sweat and blood.

Again Jesus fell to the ground, writhing in pain, stretching his aching arms wide as if they had already been nailed to the cross. But he was determined to go on to save us, so great was his love for us.

He knew that the next day he would be treated worse than an animal, shamed, ridiculed, humiliated, stripped naked before all, beaten, bloodied, murdered. On Good Friday, as on no other day in history, evil would prevail. Jesus would be abandoned, derided, and mocked outrageously, scourged, nailed to a cross, and left to die, his beautiful face covered with spittle and blood and terribly disfigured from the merciless beating.

(Recite one of the July prayers.)

Reflection for July 19

Huge, ugly thorns would be crushed down upon his head while insolent soldiers jeered him; his face would be beaten brutally until, covered with blood, it would be unrecognizable. All this, he knew in the garden, was going to happen to him. As the prophet Isaiah had proclaimed, "He was wounded for our iniquities, bruised for our sins. . . . God has laid on him the iniquity of all. . . . He shall be led like a sheep to the slaughter . . . and he shall not open his mouth."

All these things passed in pictures before his troubled mind at Gethsemani, and he was filled with a terrible sadness. But he reached down deeply into his soul and found strength to go on. While his human nature rebelled at the torture he was to endure and he was terrified at the thought of it, his love for us is so great he could not turn back. The sins of men stunned him and crushed him to the earth; piercing grief and heartache tore him in two, but he remained resolute and unvanquished. He would, like gold, go through the fire to glory.

Now in the distance Jesus could hear a confused rumble, and he knew the soldiers were coming. Standing up, he saw the glare of torches. He went to the Apostles and said, "You can sleep now and take your rest . . . the Son of Man is being betrayed into the hands of sinners. . . . Behold, the betrayer is here."

Judas led the guards in to the garden. So that they would know which one of them was Jesus, he had told them, "Whoever I kiss, that is he; hold him fast." He went straight up to Jesus and boldly kissed him, saying, "Hail, Rabbi!" Even at this last moment Jesus tried to save him. He said, "Do you betray the Son of Man with a kiss?" But the guards grabbed him and held him. Peter made a half-hearted effort to fight them off with a sword, but Jesus said, "Put away the sword. All who take up the sword shall perish by the sword."

(Recite one of the July prayers.)

Reflection for July 20

Jesus was arrested, and all the Apostles ran away. They had boldly protested how brave they would be, but when the time came for courage they were filled with fear. They had said they would defend him and even die with him, but now they fled into the night.

He was abandoned by all. He had wanted to spread the fire of love over the earth, but he was made a prisoner, even though his only crime was "going about doing good."

Jesus was manacled and brought before the High Priest. The council or Sanhedrin, the high assembly, had hastily been gathered to try him despite the fact that a night trial was illegal. By this time the Pharisees, who made up most of the Sanhedrin, were willing to do anything.

Paid-off witnesses were produced to tell lies about him. But it is hard to keep track of lies; they contradicted one another, and the trial began to fall into shambles. The leaders feared they might even have to let him go. After all, it is pretty difficult to convict a man of crime who only preaches love. But by a stroke of luck, the High Priest saved the day. He rose and asked, "Tell me, are you the Christ, the Son of God?"

Jesus could have said no. He might have replied that this was only a figure of speech, a flight of poetic fancy, and that he did not mean it to be taken literally. If he had said this, they would have had to free him. No one knew

this better than Christ. He was well aware that he was
signing his own death warrant when he said, "I am."

The High Priest, in a pretense of great anger, tore
his garments and declared Jesus guilty. The whole Council at once agreed. Thus was fulfilled Jesus' prophecy
that whoever killed the just would think he was doing a
service for God.

But the trial was not over. They had to take him to
Pilate for the governor's approval.

(Recite one of the July prayers.)

Reflection for July 21

While the trial of Jesus was taking place, Peter was
sitting in the courtyard. After fleeing, he had come back
to see what would happen. At the Last Supper he had
boasted that he would always be faithful to Christ. But
Jesus had said, "This very night, before the cock crows
twice, you will deny me three times."

In the courtyard, warming himself by a fire started
by some of the guards, Peter was asked by a maidservant
if he was a disciple of Jesus, because he also talked like a
Galilean. Peter at once denied it. Later someone asked
him again, and Peter again denied it, more vehemently.
Later still, someone said, "Surely you are one of his disciples, for you too are from Galilee." This time Peter began to curse and to swear, "I do not know the man."

Just then a rooster crowded twice. Jesus, being led
by, looked at Peter, and that single glance struck right to
his heart. He went out and wept bitterly.

Judas in the meantime also had remorse, but of another kind. He ran back to the chief priests and elders
and threw down the thirty pieces of silver. He cried out in
pain, "I have sinned in betraying innocent blood."

The leaders only sneered, and Judas went out and hanged himself. Peter sinned and turned to Christ; Judas sinned and turned to despair. Judas's real sin was not in the betrayal, bad as that was, but in believing in pride that his sin was too great for the mercy of God to forgive. Had Judas only asked, he would have been pardoned. What a tragic figure and how vainly foolish was Judas Iscariot!

By now Jesus was at the palace of Pontius Pilate, the Roman governor. The Pharisees said he must condemn this man to death.

(Recite one of the July prayers.)

Reflection for July 22

The Pharisees were very clever. In their trial they claimed Jesus was guilty of blasphemy, but they knew this would not impress Pilate, a pagan. Indeed, if they brought up this charge he would have said, "Get out of here — I don't care if he violates your silly religion." Thus before Pilate they lied in their teeth. They accused him of the very thing that he refused to do. They said he wanted to lead a rebellion against the Romans. This got the governor's attention, for the very thing he was sent out to this Godforsaken land to do was to put down revolts.

The irony of it all! The truth is that the Pharisees wanted a revolution in the worst way, but when the people tried to force Jesus to be their king and lead a revolt, he would have nothing to do with it. The Pharisees surely, then, must have almost choked on these words.

However, Pilate questioned Jesus for a few minutes and knew he was innocent. He had known these wily religious leaders to lie to him before, and it was evident now that they were up to another trick. The fact was that Pilate, clothed in the gold of Rome on an imperial throne, felt naked as he sat in judgment upon this kingly figure who stood silent and shackled before him.

All the long night Jesus had suffered in silence. He had said almost nothing before the Sanhedrin, for he knew it was a fake trial. He said little more to Pilate, a puppet political figure. Pilate, however, wanted — like many a petty politician before and after — to please everyone. He wished to let Jesus go, but in a way by which no one would be offended — an impossible task.

He tried to pass the buck. He recalled that it was the festival day and he could release a prisoner. So he went out on the balcony and offered to release Jesus or Barabbas, the most vicious criminal in prison. The people called for Barabbas. Pilate was shocked.

(Recite one of the July prayers.)

Reflection for July 23

Pilate, a Roman, despised the Jews. He did not know them and did not want to know them. It was because of this that he did not realize that the crowd below the balcony was a paid-off lynch mob assembled by the Pharisees. The good-hearted family people of Jerusalem did not know what was going on; they were home in bed. These were half-drunk, vicious winos and derelicts who would have sold out on their mother for a drink. The Pharisees sent cheerleaders into the crowd to pay them and lead them in crying out against Christ.

The religious leaders had gotten this assembly together, emptying out the cheap shelters and gathering up some moronic street people. They desperately wanted Jesus on the way to execution before the decent citizens of Jerusalem would find out. The answer the crowd gave Pilate exposed them. What family man would call for a crazed killer like Barabbas to be let out of jail?

Pilate in shock said, "What should I do with Jesus?"

They cried "Crucify him."

Pilate could not believe this. He asked, "Why? What evil has he done?" The mob, of course, had no answer, and like all demented crowds they simply shouted all the louder, "Crucify him, crucify him!"

Pilate never did seem to understand what was going on. The Pharisees did trick him, not with their words, but with the words they had the crowd call out.

Next Pilate thought of another way out. He heard that Jesus was from Galilee and Herod, the king of that district, was in Jerusalem to celebrate the festival. He would send Jesus to Herod.

When Herod heard that Jesus was on the way, he was delighted. He was a playboy having a riotous party, and this Nazarene was a magician who could entertain his guests.

(Recite one of the July prayers.)

Reflection for July 24

Herod and his jaded guests welcomed Jesus, the wonder worker, and wanted him to perform magic tricks for them. Jesus remained silent, the only possible posture in the presence of a fool. The king was embarrassed; he was used to clapping his hands and having people come running. This man did nothing.

To save the day, they dressed Jesus as a jester-ruler

and made fun of him. But they soon grew bored with this, as they did with all things, and they sent him away and summoned the dancing girls once more.

Christ was back with Pilate, who now had a third plan. He sent him to the dungeons to be beaten up by the soldiers. When he came back all bloodied, the governor was sure the people would at last have mercy on him.

Christ was returned and even Pilate gasped, for the ruffians had beaten Jesus much more than he had intended. He was covered with blood, and they had fashioned a crown of thorns and pressed it down upon his head.

Surely the crowd, when they saw all this blood and suffering, would let him go. But again we see that this was not a normal crowd. Pilate brought him out on the balcony and said, "Behold, the man."

And the crowd cried all the more, "Crucify him, crucify him!"

The governor was beside himself, at wit's end. He stood on the edge of a cliff of confusion, and then the clever Pharisees and their cohorts sent him a message that pushed him over. They said that if he freed Jesus they would report him to Rome for not punishing this revolutionary. Pilate knew the Nazarene was innocent, but this was too much. No petty politician, looking for promotion, wants to be reported.

Pilate caved in. The Pharisees had lied so often about Jesus, surely they would lie about *him*. They were devious and difficult. And just to be reported was dangerous: by the time Rome had untangled all their lies, Pilate would be an old man. The one thing he did not want was to be stuck here. And so he gave over Jesus to the soldiers to be crucified.

(Recite one of the July prayers.)

Reflection for July 25

Pilate put on a strange show on the balcony. He washed his hands and declared, "I am innocent of the blood of this man." Then, after proclaiming he was innocent, he gave him to the soldiers to murder. Justice was mocked. Jesus was to die because a little politician feared the Pharisees had influence in high places.

Christ was forced to take up his cross. His back, already bloody and torn to bits, could hardly bear the weight of his burden. He stumbled along, and more than once he fell.

Along the way he saw his beloved Mother, the person closest to him in all the world, standing along the street, her arms opened to him, tears streaming down her face. But the crude soldiers pushed her back and shoved him forward. Weeping women cried for him. He wanted to bless them, but this brought another kick from the Romans.

At last they reached the hill of execution. Here the Shepherd would lay down his life for his sheep. He was utterly exhausted. They tore off his clothes. Christ stood naked in striking contrast to the rich-robed Pharisees who hooted at him.

The butchers threw him down on the cross and nailed him to the wood. The cross was raised on Calvary hill. Abbot Marmion gives us this prayer, "O my soul, behold, your God is hanging on the cross, fulfilling the words of the prophet, 'I am a worm and no man, the reproach of men and the outcast of people.' "

The first words of Jesus from the cross were to ask forgiveness for his persecutors. Then he saw his Mother, and gave her to John, and John to her. In so doing, he gave his Mother to us, to be our Mother also. On Calvary she became the Mother not only of the Redeemer but of the redeemed. This was his final gift, one of his greatest gifts to his followers. He tells us, "Fear not, she who helped me will always help you."

(Recite one of the July prayers.)

Reflection for July 26

Mary, standing beneath the cross, seeing her Son covered with blood, could not believe that humans could be so inhuman. It was like a nightmare.

Jesus, always gracious, even in agony, pardoned the thief on his right. The criminal cried to him, "Do not forget me when you come into your kingdom." Jesus replied with words we long to hear: "This day you will be with me in paradise."

Christ then said, "I thirst," but when they gave him wine he would not drink. Was this to show that this greatest thirst was for souls? Father Gerald Vann, O.P., comments that so intense is the unquenchable thirst of God for man, the divine love becomes a beggar at the door of humanity.

He cried out, "My God, my God, why have you forsaken me?" Jesus spared himself no anguish, experiencing even the torture of being abandoned by the Father. He emptied his soul completely for us. It was a terrible time of desolation, excruciating agony both in body and in soul. He had to hang on now by sheer raw courage, but he did so, beating down the black demon of despair. Though his soul felt shattered, he soon after reaffirmed his faith in his Father, saying, "It is finished." He had accomplished the task the Father sent him to do.

His work was finished, and that of his followers was to begin. In God's gracious goodness, the disciples of

Jesus were to share in his mission of saving souls. We are to assuage his thirst by bringing souls to him. And this task is never finished.

As he hung on the cross, the Pharisees gloated. This was their strongest hour. They shouted insults and encouraged their paid rabble to do so too.

Heartsick in Gethsemani, Jesus is heartbroken on Golgatha. His brave and noble heart cannot endure further agony, and he says, "Father, into your hands I commend my spirit."

(Recite one of the July prayers.)

Reflection for July 27

Blood and water flowed from the love-broken heart pierced by the soldiers. No one can dare to look at the crucifix and say, "God does not love me." Jesus showed that he would do anything, endure anything for us. He died for every human, even the most sinful and frivolous. Even the least of the little ones is held fast in the embrace of the everlasting love of Jesus. For us he became a sacrificial victim. No matter how abandoned and obscure we are, he has a flaming, radiant love for us. By his death he lifts us up. And so in the crucifixion we grasp the splendor of God's love.

In the passion, Christ made suffering redemptive. And he told us that if we suffer we can help him save souls. "If one Christian sins, another can be holy for him," Caryll Houselander reminds us. Christ in truth taught more than that. He said that the healing service we give to one another, we give to him. "Whatever you do for the least of my little ones, you do for me," he said.

Jesus did not argue about the meaning of pain; he endured it. We humans cannot explain suffering, but we know that Jesus shared it with us. Indeed the Gospel is a record of life expressed in pain. Jesus showed us that one cannot have love without pain. His love is a burning fire, a love that is fierce and gentle, patient, devouring, and all-embracing. No one loves us like Jesus. And if we let his love enter our hearts, it burns away the dross of self-ishness.

Mary had such a love. Loyal to Jesus to the end, she stood with eyes closed in prayer. She remained on Calvary and endured the ultimate horror of seeing her Son die. As they laid his lifeless body in her arms, she thought that she would die too. She remembered the first time she had held him in the cave at Bethlehem, how thrilled in heart she had been; and now in deepest sorrow she held his murdered body in her motherly arms.

(Recite one of the July prayers.)

Reflection for July 28

Holy Saturday was the most desolate day in the history of Christianity. For the Apostles, everything they loved most dearly was gone. They were sure it was all over. They were dejected beyond words; there was no consoling them. All their instincts told them to run away again, this time for good, but they stayed because Mary was with them and her courage was so admirable. They who had deserted her Son could not desert her, at least not right away.

But the next day, Easter, Jesus returned to them to give them pardon and peace. The women had gone to the tomb early and found it empty. They rushed back to tell the Apostles, who would not believe. Peter and John went to see for themselves. The tomb was empty, it was true, but the body must have been moved, they thought.

That afternoon the eleven were in the upper room. They had the doors bolted for fear the authorities would come and put them in prison or murder them as they had killed Christ. Then suddenly Jesus stood in their midst and wished them peace. The disciples were greatly disturbed, but he calmed them and showed them the nail prints in his hands and the spear wound in his side. And then they believed and rejoiced with all their hearts. He said to them, "Receive the Holy Spirit; when you forgive sins, they are forgiven."

He who had spent so much time healing souls and forgiving sins was leaving this wondrous power in the world with his followers. Not only was sin forgiven in his day, but by means of confession it is forgiven to all people in all times. God is forever amazing in His generosity. At the Last Supper, Jesus gave us the gift of the Eucharist; in his first appearance to the Apostles on Easter, he gives us the Sacrament of Reconciliation. We cannot begin to thank him for his goodness.

As Jesus stood in the midst of his friends in the upper room, their hearts were alive with joy.

Thomas, however, was not there. When he returned, they said, "We have seen the Lord." But he would not believe.

(Recite one of the July prayers.)

Reflection for July 29

The doubting Thomas refused to believe that Jesus had risen. He said, "I will not believe unless I put my fingers into his hands and my hand into his side."

Jesus appeared again and he said to the doubter, "Come here, Thomas." Then he used the Apostle's exact words, "Put your fingers into my hands and your hand into my side, and be not unbelieving but believing."

Thomas fell to his knees and said, "My Lord and my God."

It took the Apostles a long time to realize fully the greatness of this event, but finally they were truly convinced. Our faith too is sometimes weak, and yet the Resurrection is the source of our greatest joy, for it means that Jesus is with us. We believe in the risen Christ. He has not left us; we are never alone. Here and now he is beside us, our strength in our struggle with sin. Jesus assists us today and every day: in our confusion, he gives us light; in our cowardice, he comes to us with courage; in our weariness, he gives us strength.

When Jesus was about to return to heaven, he said to his disciples, and to us, "I go to prepare a place for you, and then I will come back to take you with me, so that where I am you may also be." What wonderful words these are.

Jesus left the Apostles, and they again fell into fear. All the old dread of the authorities returned. When they could see and hear and touch Jesus, he gave them courage, but now they felt alone once more. They were no better off than before in trying to understand his message. Even after the Resurrection, one of them had asked, "Lord, are you now going to restore the dominion of Israel?" They were still looking for earthly glory, and now that he was gone, the old gloom descended on them.

(Recite one of the July prayers.)

Reflection for July 30

The Apostles remained confused and desolate in the upper room, still dull of heart and dull of mind. It was only Mary, leading them in prayer, who held them together. No wonder we call her the Mother of the Church.

And then on Pentecost everything changed. God came to earth a second time, not as man as at Christmas, but as Holy Spirit, not proposing the truth from without but instilling truth into the hearts of the Apostles from within. Truth took possession of them and all was changed. In one of the greatest miracles of all, the cowardly Apostles were suddenly brave; the confused Apostles became instantly knowledgeable.

On Pentecost the Father and Son sent their Love to humanity to energize the love of men and to renew the face of the earth. Mankind was re-created. As St. Peter wrote, we are "made alive in the Spirit." He is our vivifier and inspiration.

Father Gerald Vann, O.P. wrote, "Pentecost was the flowing back of divine life into the world." A mighty wind and fire brought light and courage to the Apostles hiding in the upper room. It made them new men. And they went out and began to preach Christ. They knew that it would mean persecution of all kinds; they did not care. They spread out to the four winds to tell everyone who would listen, everyone of good will, the good news that Jesus had brought to earth.

The message of Jesus was soon known everywhere. It spread like a prairie fire across the ancient world. From the teaching of a handful of men, Christianity became the religion of thousands, then hundreds of thousands. Beyond all belief, people gave up the easy life of paganism and accepted the hard teachings of Christ.

Wherever the early Christians went, the Holy Spirit

guided them and gave them ever greater faith, hope, and love.

(Recite one of the July prayers.)

Reflection for July 31

With the early Christians we pray, "Come, Holy Spirit." We beg Him for the light and courage to be noble followers of Christ, as he gave these gifts to the Apostles. We ask Him who brought life to the early Church to give new life to us, to revitalize our lackluster spirits. May He support us as He did the Apostles and sustain us and comfort us and be our Advocate.

We ask the Holy Spirit to cleanse our hearts and enlighten our dull minds so that our souls will be fertile for Christ to be fully formed within us.

Often we feel shriveled in soul. May the Holy Spirit help us. With light and zeal let Him give us new spirit, for He is the fountain of leaping love and the fire that can set us ablaze.

Come Holy Spirit, for we find it difficult to resist the strength of the enemy unleashed against us.

Come, Father of the poor, Giver of every good gift, Light of all minds; come, Comforter, refresh us, console us, set straight what has gone crooked, and fill our arid souls with your love.

All these blessings we pray for now were given to the Apostles on Pentecost. Their hearts were so filled with love they could not resist going out and telling people about Jesus. In him, they said, was eternal life. "Salvation is not found elsewhere," they stated. This was the beginning of the Church. Pentecost is its birthday. The Church in every age preaches Christ, just as the first

Apostles reached out to others with the love of the Lord.

The message of Jesus, thought by the Pharisees to be snuffed out on Good Friday, spread far and wide. Christ triumphed. Even though the authorities continued to persecute the Christians, murdering many, the faith could not be destroyed, any more than Jesus could be destroyed. Why? Because Jesus is with us, just as he promised to be, even until the end of the world.

(Recite one of the July prayers.)

Prayers for July

O Precious Blood of Jesus shed for me, wash me. I am sorry that my sins caused such agony on the cross. You, Jesus, are the most tender, most affectionate, the holiest of all those who have walked in the world. And yet you died like a criminal because you wished to show me that you love me so much you are willing to do anything for me, even to suffering the terrible, horrible agony of crucifixion. From the cross, at the end, you gave yourself into the hands of the Father. I put myself in your hands. I hope and pray that with your grace I will live a good life so that you will not have died in vain. Amen.

Lord, you have a special love for the sick. Bless, please, those who are ill, and especially those who are near and dear to us. Hold them in your arms and heal them. Comfort them with your great and unfailing love. Grant them your saving grace. Come, Jesus, and console them with your love and mercy. Free them from harm and suffering. Bless those dedicated to the care of the sick. Bear the weakness of the poor in health and carry away their sorrow, you who went among the people doing good and healing the sick. Amen.

Bless all children, we beseech you, dearest Jesus, and especially those of our family. Give parents wisdom and love so that homes may be more like your loving home with Mary and Joseph in Nazareth. O Lord, remember homeless and unwanted children, the children of loveless homes, children who are mistreated, and those who are ill. Protect them and care for them, for they are your special love. You said, "Let the little children come to me." Watch over them, Christ Jesus. For this we pray. Amen.

O heavenly Father, in whom we live and move and have our being, we humbly pray that you will guide and govern us this day and every day, so that in all our cares and occupations we may always love you and always walk in your sight. O Lord God, from whom neither life nor death can separate those who trust in your love, and whose love holds and embraces us, your dear children, unite us to you, give us courage and constancy. We ask this through Jesus, who shed his Precious Blood for us. Amen.

Lord Jesus, I so often forget you. I get busy about many things. Help me to remember that you are the most important thing. I want you to know that I have a grateful heart for all the support you have given me. Let me pray more and spend less time in worry. I commend into your hands my loved ones, living and dead. Strengthen those who are weak, confirm the faithful, give heart and hope to sinners, give peace to the dying, and guide the perplexed. Amen.

Dearest Lord, watch over those who are weeping, give hope to the hopeless, give inspiration to the careless. Bless all poor sinners. Tend the sick, O Lord Christ, rest the weary, soothe the suffering, pity the afflicted, shield the young. We are all, each and every one, in need of your graces. Help us to do all things for your love's sake.

We bring before you all those whom we love, knowing that you love them even more than we do. Grant them courage to follow in your footsteps all the day long.

Where shall we go, if you will not help us? But we trust in
your words, Lord, and know that you will indeed come to
our assistance. Amen.

Lord Jesus, give grace to us and our family and
friends, to our neighbors, and to all in need. May we
serve you, O Christ, in one another, and love as you love
us. Comfort and heal those who suffer in body, mind, and
soul; give them courage and hope in their troubles and
bring them to the joy of your salvation. Hear us as we remember our dear ones who have died; have mercy on all
the poor souls in purgatory and grant them a share in
your eternal kingdom of love, rejoicing with the saints. O
Lord Jesus, grant us also this happiness. We commend
ourselves and all Christians to your unfailing love. Amen.

God is almighty, all wise, all good. He is rest indeed;
let us rest in Him. Jesus, of your goodness, give us yourself. You are so generous. Heal the quarrels of people
and bring families who are divided back together again.
We pray earnestly for peace with one another; we pray
that your peace may bring tranquillity to our souls.

Dear Jesus, light every heart; set free those who are
doubtful and give them a stronger faith. Let the knowledge of you fill every mind and soul. Increase our love for
others and especially for our own family. We trust you,
Lord Jesus, as we pray with humble and sincere hearts.
Amen.

My thanks, O holy Lord, for your divine mercy that
has kept me safe. O Jesus, source of every good, let your
grace flow ceaselessly into my soul. Teach us to trust you
more and to be grateful for your bountiful mercy. Give
me grace, O Lord, to be strong in all things, prudent,
just and wise. Grant me a greater faith, unshakable

confidence in you, and a more compassionate considera-
tion of others. Take my selfishness from me. I wish always to be devoted to you and to imitate you.

You, Jesus, are unspeakable joy. Make us wholly
yours so that nothing may separate us from you. Amen.

I trust in you, O Lord, and seek you with a simple
heart. You alone, Jesus, are most faithful. You will not
forsake those who believe in you. There is none other like
you. How kind and wise you are, how gracious and generous. You do not fail to give strength in the struggle and
help those in danger. You comfort us in our afflictions,
you are merciful to those who repent, and you give perseverance to those who pray.

Help all who seek you, Christ Jesus; be our support.
My Lord, my joy, you bid us to pray to you for your assistance. I turn to you in my many needs and know that
you will not fail me. Amen.

I thank you, Jesus, for watching over me. Bless me
this day, kind and tender Lord. Grant that I may live with
you; give me greater patience, understanding, and peace
of soul.

I thank you for having protected and preserved me,
for giving me health and endurance; grant that I may be
more devoted to you. Aided by your grace, let me love
you more and dedicate my day to you — you who have
done so much for me and are my dearest Friend. May
this be so, O my Jesus, through your most gentle heart.
Amen.

O God, in your sight every soul may well fear and every conscience tremble; be gracious to us sinners. Hear
our cry for help. Heal our wounds. None of us is free from
fault, so may none of us be strangers to your mercy.

It is not because of any human merits that we are

your children. This is your glorious gift to us. Protect your children, O God, our Father; guard us and guide us. Like wayward little kids, we are stubborn and thoughtless, contrary and childish. Rescue us from our willful ways; like the gracious Father that you are, take us up into your loving arms and carry us, for we are weak. Thank you, Father. Amen.

Give us the grace, O God, to love you and praise you more. With the heavenly dew of your blessings, quench our pride and passions. We need the gift of your blessings so that we may be more prayerful and devout, more loving and enlightened. Increase our faith and hope.

O Jesus, most tender, most desirable and delightful, please listen to our plea. We pray for your mercy; look with pity upon us, for we are weak and wayward souls. Wash away our guilt and give us forgiveness. Banish evil, heal our hearts, enlighten our minds, and direct our ways. Amen.

Dear Jesus, in praying for my family and friends and relatives, I know that you love them even more than I do. Please take care of them. Look after them, Lord, day and night. Bless all of us. You are so kind. You spent your days "going about doing good." And so I look to you, Christ Jesus, to help us, for there is nowhere else to look. You are our dearest Friend, you are our closest Companion as we walk through life. Help us in our sickness and troubles, our worries and trials. We need your assistance. We are weak and weary. We desire to follow you, but sometimes the struggle overcomes us. Know that we love you; help us to love you more. Amen.

All through the day, O Lord, let me touch the lives of others for good, whether by prayer or word or deed. Help

me to help someone else this day. Do not let me worry
about myself or waste my time thinking always of myself. How contrary to your spirit that is. You were forever thinking of others and helping them. And I am supposed to be Christlike. There is no other way of being a
Christian. Enlighten me to see the needs of my neighbors. Come to me, dear Christ, and fill my heart with
your love so that it may overflow and I may give some of
your love away. Surely that is what you wish me to do
more than anything. But for this I need your blessings.
Guide me in your way. Amen.

Show us your loving kindness this day, Lord Jesus.
Grant your graces to all who stand in need of help. Be
with the weak and make them strong, and with the strong
and make them gentle. Cheer the lonely, prosper your
people, give peace to families and love to hearts; refresh
the weary who have toiled all the day. Give light to the
darkness of souls in sin, and bless especially all who are
sick and dying and the poor souls in purgatory.

Be with me today, Lord Jesus, keep me free from
harm and danger; please grant me your precious grace
in time of temptation and difficulty; help me to grow in
being more like you. I am so impatient with myself; do
not, please, Lord, lose patience with me. I pray that we,
your followers, may all grow together in you and with
you. Amen.

I entreat your mercy, Jesus, for my family and loved
ones, living and dead. Please bless all families, all hus-
bands and wives, all children. Be in every heart and
home. Hallow our homes with your gift of goodness. Let
there be peace in families, kindness and love and
courtesy. Be with each family, especially in time of need,
in sickness, trouble, and sorrow. We cannot endure with-

out you. Humbly we beg your loving assistance. Guide us
with your wisdom, show us your way, and give us the
courage to follow you. Amen.

O God, all things in heaven and on earth are yours. I
offer myself to you. In the simplicity of my heart I give
you this gift. Let me be your servant today and serve you
by serving my neighbor. In this way I hope to make up for
my sins. Consume me with your goodness, dear Lord, so
that I may do good for others.

I ask your grace today for parents, friends, brothers,
sisters, all my loved ones, living and dead. I come to you
because I love you and need you. I am unhappy without
you; your grace is my support. I seek you because I know
no one loves me as you do. May I never lose your friendship. May I follow you and strive to serve you to my dying
day. Amen.

O Lord, you know my heart, you know that I love you.
Everything I have you have given to me, and I am grateful. Let me learn from you to be more gracious and generous. Teach me, Jesus, for you are my guide and I need
your good counsel. Encourage me, Lord, for I am weak
with human frailty. Be merciful, my Jesus, for I am in
need. My faith is mediocre, my love is lukewarm. Give
me the grace to grow spiritually, to trust you more, to
help others more. Support me, Lord; alone, I cannot be a
real Christian. Rid me of my languor, my spiritual sickness, my feebleness of soul, my irritability. Give me a
proper, more spiritual view of life; I am too earthbound,
too materialistic. Give me courage and humility in all
things, and above all, please give me your undying love.
Amen.

I know that if in all things I seek you, Jesus, I will
find you. I realize that if I truly know you, dear Friend, I

will love you. Why, then, do I fail to seek you, to know you? It is my laziness, my love of comfort, my desire for pleasure, my spending too much time being entertained. And so I take on worldly ways, and the world ignores you, Jesus. Help me to pray more, to be with you more, to visit you more. Help me to be less proud and more humble, to beg for your heavenly wisdom so that I may cast aside the false philosophy of the world. Let me love you more dearly, and I will truly know how to live. Amen.

Almighty God, Father of mercies, we are your unworthy servants. We most humbly and heartily thank you for your goodness and loving kindness. We are grateful to you for creating us, for preserving us and all the blessings in this life. We especially are appreciative that you sent your Son to rescue us by his death on the cross for our redemption.

Please bless the homeless and the hungry, those suffering exile, the refugees, and people imprisoned in nations ruled by dictators.

Grant us peace on earth, that we may all live together as a family, each caring for all, all caring for each, for the sake of tranquillity. O God of peace, and Jesus, the Prince of Peace, grant our prayer. Amen.

Comfort, we beseech you, most gracious God, all who are cast down, the faint of heart and those in sorrow. Lift them up, Lord. Glory to you, O God, Creator and Father, for all the good things you have given us. Grant to us, Lord, a humble spirit. Make us tender and compassionate toward others. We look ever to you for grace. Preserve us by your goodness and mercy to the end. Be master of our hearts and minds. Lord God almighty, we are unworthy, but you have made us your children. God of all mercy and love, help us to be wise and understanding, so that one day we may rejoice with you in your glorious heavenly kingdom. Amen.

Dearest Jesus, receive our prayers and supplications. Bless us, for we need you. Salvation is through the Precious Blood. Our Redeemer, you washed away our iniquity with your most Precious Blood. We pray to be set on fire with the flames which you, O Jesus, came to kindle. Through your Precious Blood, grace comes to us, and our hearts burn within. By suffering the crucifixion, you piled high your blessings for us, Lord Jesus. This is the dew of your kingdom of love, and we are deeply grateful. Amen.

Deliver us, O God, from following the fashions of the day in our thinking. Free us from doing things because they are popular. Save us from foolish living, as though this world were the only world. Do not let us abuse the talents you have given us by devoting ourselves chiefly to making money. Help us never to confuse the toys and trinkets of this life with the glory of the life to come. Keep our minds straight. Free us from putting all our hope in the things of earth. Let us always remember that Jesus is our guide and our salvation is through him. Amen.

O Christ, the keeper of us all, stretch out your hand and protect us day and night. Take care of me and my loved ones, for only you can guard us from evil. I give myself and my family entirely into your keeping. I know that you will provide for all our needs today and always.

All things we have in soul and body, and whatever else we possess, you, dear Friend, have lovingly given to us. We are glad and grateful and thank you very much. Assist us each day so that we can do your bidding, so that we can show your gracious love to others. You have been so bountiful, loving, and good to us. Help us to help you by loving our neighbors. Amen.

Cardinal Newman's Meditation

Whatever, wherever I am, I can never be thrown away. If I am in sickness, my sickness may serve Jesus; in perplexity, my perplexity may serve him; if I am in sorrow, my sorrow may serve him. My sickness, or perplexity or sorrow may be necessary causes of some great end, which is beyond us. He does nothing in vain; he may prolong my life, he may shorten it; he knows what he is about. He may take away my friends. He may throw me among strangers. He may make me feel desolate, make my spirits sink, hide the future from me — still he knows what he is about. . . . I trust you wholly. You are wiser than I — more loving to me than I myself. Deign to fulfill your high purposes in me, whatever they may be — work in and through me. I am born to serve you; to be yours, to be your instrument. Let me be your blind instrument. I ask not to see — I ask not to know — I ask simply to be used.

Litany of the Most Precious Blood

Lord, have mercy on us.
Christ, have mercy on us.
Lord, have mercy on us.
Christ, hear us.
Christ, graciously hear us.
God, the Father of Heaven, *have mercy on us.**

God, the Son, Redeemer of the World,*
God, the Holy Spirit,*
Holy Trinity, one God,*
Blood of Christ, only-begotten Son of the Eternal Father,
    save us.†
Blood of Christ, Word of God†
Blood of Christ, of the New and Eternal Testament,
Blood of Christ, falling upon the earth in the agony,
Blood of Christ, shed profusely in the scourging,
Blood of Christ, flowing forth in the crowning with
    thorns,
Blood of Christ, price of our salvation,
Blood of Christ, poured out on the cross,
Blood of Christ, without which there is no forgiveness,
Blood of Christ, Eucharistic drink and refreshment of
    souls,
Blood of Christ, stream of mercy,
Blood of Christ, victory over demons,
Blood of Christ, courage of martyrs,
Blood of Christ, strength of confessors,
Blood of Christ, bringing forth virgins,
Blood of Christ, help of those in peril,
Blood of Christ, relief of the burdened,
Blood of Christ, solace in sorrow,
Blood of Christ, hope of penitents,
Blood of Christ, consolation of the dying,
Blood of Christ, peace and tenderness of hearts,
Blood of Christ, pledge of Eternal Life,
Blood of Christ, freeing souls from Purgatory,
Blood of Christ, most worthy of all glory and honor,
Lamb of God, who take away the sin of the world, spare
    us, O Lord.

Have mercy on us is repeated after each invocation.
†*Save us* is repeated after each invocation.

Lamb of God, who take away the sin of the world,
  graciously hear us, O Lord.
Lamb of God, who take away the sin of the world, have
  mercy on us.
V. You have redeemed us, O Lord, in your Blood,
R. And made us, for our God, a kingdom.

Let us Pray

Almighty and Eternal God, You have appointed your
only begotten Son the Redeemer of the world, and will to
be appeased by his Blood; grant, we beg you, that we
may worthily adore this price of our salvation, and
through its power be safeguarded from the evils of this
present life, so that we may rejoice in its fruits forever in
heaven. We ask this through Christ our Lord. Amen.

III. EVER Rejoice! Jesus Is Here!

Maxims and meditations on life, death, and eternity; on Christ, and living as a Christian

Throughout the year, with the help of the saints and Scriptures, we reflect on the eternal verities and the glorious implications of Jesus' resurrection.

Wisdom of the Saints

After Jesus, no one can tell us better than the saints about life and death and their meaning. Worldly wisdom cannot guide us in truly important matters. We must look to the wisdom of the holy men and women who have walked in the world before us.

WHAT IS GOD LIKE?

God is a being eternal and omnipotent. — St. Bonaventure.

The heavens show forth the glory of God, and the earth declares the work of His hands. — *The Psalms.*

We cannot know God in His greatness, for the Father cannot be measured. — St. Irenaeus.

God's mercies are infinite. — St. John Chrysostom.

God can never be sought in vain. — St. Bernard of Clairvaux.

God dispenses His mercy with a beneficent hand.
— St. Francis de Sales.

The Almighty does nothing without reason, though the frail mind of man cannot explain the reason. — St. Augustine.

The greatest and most regal work of God is the salvation of humanity   — St. Clement of Alexandria.

God dwells in a secret and hidden way in all souls.
                              — St. John of the Cross.

Whither shall anyone go away, or where shall anyone run away from God, who embraces the whole universe?
                              — St. Clement of Rome.

God is compassionate and merciful, will forgive sins in the day of tribulation . . . a protector to all that seek Him in truth. — *Sirach (Ecclesiasticus)*.

God loved the world so much that He gave His only begotten Son, so that anyone who believes in him may not perish but may have eternal life. — St. John.

I am the Lord, and I change not. — *Malachi* (Old Testament prophet).

DOES GOD LOVE US?
God takes care of all existing things. — St. John Damascene.

If God is on our side, who can be against us? — St. Paul (in *Romans*).

God's goodness will take care of me; His gracious help will supply my lack. — St. Thomas More (in prison, comforting his daughter).

The Lord's mercy may be found between bridge and river. — St. Augustine (in speaking of someone who had committed suicide jumping off a bridge).

If there be anyone who, seeing all around us the works of God, does not praise Him — he is stupid. — St. Bonaventure.

In the morning, when the sun rises, all men ought to praise God, who created all for our use. — St. Francis of Assisi.

The first dictate of reason is the kindling in us of love and reverence for the Divine Majesty, to whom we owe both all we have and all that we can ever hope for. — St. Thomas More.

If God withdrew His power from us, we would have no more being than we had before we were created. — St. Augustine.

You are the Holy Lord God, who alone works marvels. You are beautiful, defender, gentleness, sweetness and eternal life. — St. Francis of Assisi.

God guards us among the savages with so much love. He gives such abundant consolations, in the trials we have to endure, that we do not even think of regretting what we have renounced for His sake. — St. Isaac Jogues, S.J. (telling of early missionary life among the American Indians).

WHO SHOULD GUIDE US IN LIFE?
This Jesus whom you crucified . . . there is salvation in no other. — St. Peter (in *Acts*).

The Son of God was made the Son of man that the children of man might be made children of God. — St. Athanasius.

Lord, to whom shall we go? You have the words of eternal life. — St. Peter (in *John 6*).

DOES JESUS WANT TO HELP US?
I am ready to die for you — I love you so much.
— Jesus (paraphrase of *John 10, 13-15*).

I came that they should have life, and have it more abundantly. — Jesus (*John 10*).

His hands are stretched out to gather all men together. — St. Irenaeus.

Christ is a king who will provide for you; he will give you in abundance all that can make you happy. — St. Edmund Campion.

WHAT IS MAN?
He is a rational soul and a mortal body. — St. Augustine.

All people equally bear in themselves the divine image. — St. Gregory of Nyssa.

Since the human soul cannot be produced by the changing of matter, it must be produced immediately by God. — St. Thomas Aquinas.

What is your life? It is a vapor that appears for a little time and then vanishes. — St. James.

As sure as I lived, I knew that I possessed a will, and that when I willed to do something or willed not to do something, nobody else was making that decision. — St. Augustine.

Let us make man to our image and likeness. — The words of God in *Genesis 1*.

HOW SHOULD WE LIVE?

Found not your hope on yourself but on God. — St. Augustine.

To those who love God, all things work together unto good. — St. Paul (in *Romans*).

By this will all men know that you are my disciples, that you have love for one another. — Jesus (in *John 13*).

Our Lord does not care so much for the importance of our works as for the love with which they are done.
                                        — St. Teresa of Avila.

WHAT IS OUR GOAL IN LIFE?

Man is born to have a rendezvous with God. He is made for the contemplation of heaven. — St. Clement of Alexandria.

All things, by desiring their own perfection, desire God himself. — St. Thomas Aquinas.

God has granted to those who follow Him and serve Him life and incorruption and eternal glory. — St. Irenaeus.

Let your desire be to see God and your joy be for what will lead you to Him. — St. Teresa of Avila.

Many men will cross the sea for gain, enduring at least as much as we; and shall we not, for God's love, do what others do for worldly ends? — St. Isaac Jogues (missionary to American Indians).

WHAT DOES GOD WANT US TO DO?

Let each one remember that he will make progress in all spiritual things only insofar as he rids himself of self-love, self-will, and selfish interests. — St. Ignatius Loyola.

No duty is more urgent than that of returning thanks to God. — St. Ambrose.

Love is from God. Everyone who loves is of God and knows God. He who does not love does not know God — for God is Love. — St. John.

HOW DOES A GOOD CHRISTIAN ACT?

It is in pardoning that we are pardoned. — Anon. (*Prayer of St. Francis*).

A mild answer turns away anger. . . . — The Bible (*Proverbs*).

Patience is the companion of wisdom. — St. Augustine.

WHY BE HUMBLE?

Christ is with those of humble heart. — St. Clement of Rome.

Humility is the royal gateway through which one approaches the inner court of Christ. — St. John Climacus.

Without humility, all is lost. — St. Teresa of Avila.

Keep your eyes off other people's faults and fix them on your own. — St. Alphonsus Liguori.

Holy men, the higher they raise themselves, approaching to God, the more clearly do they perceive their own unworthiness. — St. Gregory the Great.

Three things are needed for learning, the first is humility, the second is humility and the third is humility.
                                        — St. Augustine.

Lord, do not trust Philip; he will betray you. — St. Philip Neri.

Pride changed angels into devils; humility makes men into angels. — St. Augustine.

DO WE NEED GOD'S GRACE?
Do not try to persuade yourself that you can do anything good on your own. — St. Ignatius of Antioch.

It is grace alone that separates the good from the bad. Grace conquers sin. — St. Augustine.

The grace of Christ clothes us with beauty. — St. Cyril of Alexandria.

I am at the most the one who sows the seeds and waters them, but then what would I have done without the One who makes them grow? — St. Bernard of Clairvaux.

Grace is the beginning of glory in us. — St. Thomas Aquinas.

O God, I have no hope at all but in your great mercy. — St. Augustine.

Grace sets me free from the slavery of sin. — St. Bernard of Clairvaux.

My grace is sufficient for you. — God to St. Paul (*2 Corinthians*).

ARE WE TO HELP OTHERS?

When you see your brother, you see Christ. — St. Clement of Alexandria.

In proportion as you advance in brotherly love, you are increasing your love for God. — St. Teresa of Avila.

To love your neighbor is to love God in man and man in God. — St. Francis de Sales.

Let one in gentleness and mercy direct another on his way. — St. Basil.

That money will be more profitable to you that you give to the poor. — St. Ambrose.

Anyone who says, "I love God," yet hates his brother — he is a liar. — St. John.

One furthers his own love by loving others. — St. Augustine.

Bear one another's burdens. . . . — St. Paul (in *Galatians*).

Mercy imitates God. — St. John Chrysostom.

Give aid to the poor and do not inquire how good they are. — St. Ambrose.

The bread that you store up belongs to the poor. — St. Basil.

There will be no mercy to those who have shown no mercy. — St. James.

And the king . . . shall say to them, "Amen . . . as long as you did it to one of these my least brethren, you did it to me." — Jesus (in *Matthew 25*).

HOW CAN WE BE HAPPY?
All the way to heaven is heaven. — St. Catherine of Siena.

Have no anxiety about anything, but . . . by prayer . . . present your requests to God. — St. Paul in *Philippians*).

It is in giving that we receive. — Anon. (*Prayer of St. Francis*).

Let not your hearts be troubled. — Jesus (in *John 14*).

Though things are difficult, do not feel sad. We are not alone. God our Father is with us. — St. Francis of Assisi.

WERE THE SAINTS HAPPY?
God has changed all our sunsets to sunrise. — St. Clement of Alexandria.

A sad saint would be a sorry saint. — St. Francis de Sales.

Where there is sadness, let me bring joy. — Anon. (*Prayer of St. Francis*).

When we serve with joy we promote the honor and glory of God. — St. Alphonsus Rodriguez.

Let the Brothers take care that they do not present the appearances of hypocrites, with dark and downcast mien, but that they show themselves glad in the Lord, cheerful and worthy of love and agreeable. — St. Francis of Assisi.

Every creature of God is good, and nothing to be rejected that is received with thanksgiving. — St. Paul (in *1 Timothy*).

DID THE SAINTS HAVE A SENSE OF HUMOR?

Dear Lord, if this is the way you treat your friends, no wonder you have so few of them. — St. Teresa of Avila (when thrown from her horse).

I hope that none of his other friends might experience a like mercy of the king. — St. Thomas More (when told that since he was a friend of Henry VIII, he would not be hanged and quartered but only have his head cut off).

I am perfectly sure that he would much rather have a good laugh than be occupied with things at court, no matter how high they are. — Erasmus (speaking of St. Thomas More, the Lord Chancellor of England).

The Devil, being a proud spirit, cannot endure to be mocked. — St. Thomas More.

I pray you help me up — as for my coming down, you

can let me shift for myself. — St. Thomas More (to a soldier, concerning the stairs to the platform where he was to be beheaded).

SHOULD A CHRISTIAN LOVE THE WORLD?
It is good. — God, after creating the world (*Genesis 1*).

If there be any man who is not enlightened by the sublime magnificence of nature, he is blind. — St. Bonaventure.

Beauty is God's daughter. — St. Francis of Assisi.

The trees and nature will teach you that which you cannot hear from masters; you shall find fuller satisfaction in the woods than in books. — St. Bernard of Clairvaux.

Man should admire not only the ingenuity of nature but the wisdom of the Creator. — St. Robert Bellarmine.

Praised be my Lord God with all His creatures, and especially our brother the sun, who brings us the light, fair is he who shines with a very great splendor; praised be my Lord for our sister the moon, and for the stars, which He has set clear and lovely in heaven; praised be my Lord for our brother the wind and for the air and clouds, for our sister water and brother fire and for our mother the earth, who sustains us and keeps us and brings forth diverse fruits and flowers of many colors.
— St. Francis of Assisi.

WHAT SHOULD WE AVOID?
The Christian should fear nothing so much as separation from Christ. — St. Augustine.

There are some fools so fed with the fond fantasy of fame that they rejoice and glory to think how they are continually praised all about. — St. Thomas More.

Idleness is the enemy of the soul. — St. Benedict.

Pride is the infernal serpent that creeps into moral breasts. — St. Thomas More.

Ambition is a secret poison; it is an evil crucifying and disquieting all that it takes hold of. — St. Bernard of Clairvaux.

The soul will never find peace and happiness in worldly enjoyment. God alone can make us perfectly happy. — St. Alphonsus Liguori.

Envy is an evil sorrow at the welfare of our neighbor.
                              — St. John Baptist de la Salle.

Do not be quick to anger, for anger lodges in the bosom of fools. — *Ecclesiastes*.

Drunkenness is the ruin of reason. It is premature old age. It is temporary death. — St. Basil.

God deliver us from those who serve Him and think of their own dignity. — St. Terese of Avila.

I am sorrier for your perjury than for my peril. — St. Thomas More (to a false witness at his treason trial).

Pride is detested in the sight of the Lord. — *Ecclesiastes*.

Who can for very shame desire to enter into the Kingdom of Christ with ease, when Christ himself entered
into it not without pain? — St. Thomas More.

HOW SHOULD WE PRAY?
A spirit united to God in prayer and love acquires
wisdom, goodness, strength, benevolence and greatness
of soul. — St. Maximus the Confessor.

Prayer consists not in much thinking but in much loving. — St. Teresa of Avila.

I do as a little child who cannot read — I just say
what I want to say to God, quite simply, and He never
fails to understand. — St. Thérèse (the Little Flower).

We should pray to the angels, for they are given us as
guardians. — St. Ambrose.

What time is so holy as the time of prayer, in which
we speak with God? — St. Isaac of Nineveh.

Prayer is the source of our progress toward God.
                                        — St. Bonaventure.

Prayer is the unfolding of one's will to God that He
may fulfill it. — St. Thomas Aquinas.

One may not be given up to prayer so as to neglect
the good of his neighbor, nor so taken up with the active
life as to omit prayer to God. — St. Augustine.

After baptism, we need continual prayer in order to
enter heaven. — St. Thomas Aquinas.

When we cannot pray but continue to try, God is pleased even with our silence and patience. — St. Francis de Sales.

The simple expression of the publican in the Gospel, "God be merciful to me, a sinner," was sufficient to open the floodgates of divine compassion. — St. John Climacus.

Take from me, good Lord, this lukewarmness, my cold manner of meditation, this dullness in praying to you, and give me warmth, delight and brightness in thinking of you. — St. Thomas More.

Let a person never cease from prayer, even if his life be wicked, for prayer is the way to amend evil. — St. Teresa of Avila.

Prayer is conversation with God. — St. Clement of Alexandria.

God delights in the prayers of His people. — The Bible (*Proverbs*).

We are always in the presence of God, yet it seems to me that those who pray are in His presence in a very different sense. — St. Teresa of Avila.

We pray in the Church, in the unity of Christ's body, which body of Christ consists of the many in the whole world who believe. — St. Augustine.

IS LEARNING NECESSARY FOR SANCTITY?
Learned men can often ruin everything. Brother Francis confounded the heretics by kneeling in the mud.

His simple preaching, from his heart, has converted more than all the learned men put together. — A companion of St. Francis of Assisi.

Dear God, our knowledge compared with yours is ignorance. — St. Augustine.

I praise you, Father, Lord of heaven and earth, for hiding these things from the wise and prudent and revealing them to the little ones! — Jesus (in *Matthew*).

God's foolishness is wiser than men. . . . — St. Paul (in *1 Corinthians*).

WHAT IS SIN?

Sin is the unfaithfulness of man to the image of what he ought to be. My soul is like a mirror in which the glory of God is reflected, but sin covers the mirror with fog.
                                           — St. Teresa of Avila.

Sin, the sad fearful winter of the soul, kills the goodness which it finds there. — St. Francis de Sales.

The joy of the godless is but for a moment — The Bible (*Job*).

When man sins he acts against reason. He thereby can easily become a slave of sin and lose his liberty.
                                           — St. Thomas Aquinas.

Sin is nothing, and men become nothing when they sin. Every sin is more injury to him who does it than him who suffers it. — St. Augustine.

Sin is energy in the wrong channel. — St. Augustine.

Where is the foolish person who would think it is in his power to sin more than God can forgive? — St. Francis de Sales.

All have sinned and fallen short of the goodness of God. — St. Paul (in *Romans*).

To sin is human, but to persevere in sin is not human but altogether evil. — St. John Chrysostom.

While sinning I was fighting against myself. — St. Augustine.

WHAT IS TEMPTATION?

A thousand temptations do not make a sin. — St. Augustine.

All the temptations in hell cannot sully a soul which does not accept them. — St. Francis de Sales.

An expert seaman is tried in a tempest, a runner in a race, a captain in battle, a valiant man in adversity, a Christian in temptation. — St. Basil.

The fire of charity, thrown in the devil's face, strikes him suddenly so blind that he cannot see to strike us.
— St. Thomas Aquinas.

God is faithful and will not suffer you to be tempted above that which you are able. — St. Paul.

DOES SUFFERING HAVE A PURPOSE?

Oh, good and sweet Jesus, where were you while my soul was being sorely tormented? — St. Catherine of Siena (after being troubled. Christ replied, "I was in your heart, Catherine, for I will not leave anyone who does not leave me'').

Wheat is not separated except by threshing, and man is separated from worldly ways by tribulation. — St. John Chrysostom.

Lord, help me, so that I can bear my sickness with patience. — St. Francis of Assisi (when dying).

We always find that those who walked closest to Christ our Lord were those who had to bear the greatest trials. —St. Teresa of Avila.

God sometimes breaks people to make them anew.
                                    — St. Francis of Assisi

Many are the afflictions of the righteous, but the Lord delivers him out of them all. — *The Psalms*.

Suffering for love of God is better than working miracles. — St. John of the Cross.

Everyone knows how to be resigned amid the joys of life, but to be so amid the storms and tempests is peculiar to the children of God. — St. Francis de Sales.

Unload all your care on him [the Lord], for he has care of you. — St. Peter.

Tribulation teaches you; it does not destroy you. — St. Isidore of Seville.

WHAT SHOULD OUR ATTITUDE BE TOWARD WEALTH?

The rich man is not one who is in possession of much, but one who gives much. — St. John Chrysostom.

It is not a sin to have riches, but it is a sin to fix our hearts upon them. — St. John Baptist de la Salle.

Always abhor money — the chief cause of corruption for the clergy. Whoever does not crave riches is rich.
— St. Francis of Assisi.

Silly people think that money is the thing most worth having. — St. Thomas Aquinas.

Trust in your money and down you go. Trust in God and flourish as a tree. — The Bible (*Proverbs*).

How difficult it is to pray in prosperity. When men are wealthy and well at their ease, good God, how many mad ways our minds wander. — St. Thomas More.

Worldly friends are much worse in drawing man from God than are His mortal enemies. — St. Thomas More.

SHOULD WE TRY TO BE PEACEMAKERS?

Blessed are the peacemakers, for they shall be called the children of God. — Jesus (in *Matthew*).

Blessed are they who peaceably shall endure, for you, O most High, shall give them a crown. Praised be God for all those who pardon one another for His love's sake. — St. Francis of Assisi.

Let us therefore blush when we ourselves perversely become wolves to our foes. As soon as we become wolves we are beaten. The Shepherd leaves us. He feeds sheep, not wolves. — St. John Chrysostom.

We have changed our swords into ploughshares; we promote the love of man. — St. Justin Martyr.

ARE WE TO GROW IN SOUL?
The splendor of God is man fully realized. — St. Irenaeus.

A person is ready to flower into his potential glory, if one lets oneself enter the struggle. — St. Teresa of Avila.

Take from me my lukewarmness, Lord. — St. Thomas More.

It is not those who commit the least faults who are the most holy, but those who have the greatest courage, the greatest love, the greatest generosity, who make the boldest efforts to overcome themselves and are not immoderately apprehensive of tripping. — St. Francis de Sales.

I have learned in whatever state I am, to be content.
— St. Paul (to the *Philippians*).

SHOULD WE READ THE BIBLE?
All Scripture, inspired by God, is profitable. . . .
— St. Paul (in 2 *Timothy*).

He who is ignorant of Scripture is ignorant of Christ.
— St. Jerome.

As in paradise, God walks in the Holy Scripture seeking man. — St. Ambrose.

These words give us a sure medicine. — St. Thomas More.

The Bible is the Spirit of God speaking to us. — St. Augustine.

IS WORK A BLESSING?

Christ moves among the pots and pans. — St. Teresa of Avila.

Unemployment is an enemy to spiritual health. — St. Benedict.

Our Lord cares for our work but even more for the love with which it is done. — St. Teresa of Avila.

All Brothers should labor, be strong in the face of hardship, and have holy cheerfulness. — St. Francis of Assisi.

HOW CAN WE GET ALONG WITH OTHERS?

You can attract more flies with a spoonful of honey than with a barrel of vinegar. — St. Francis de Sales.

If you wish to be obeyed, you must appear not to be giving orders. — St. Philip Neri.

The heart of the wise seeks instruction, and the mouth of fools feeds on foolishness. — the Bible (*Proverbs*).

DO WE NEED THE CHURCH?

The Church is the society of the faithful, of whom Jesus is the invisible Head. — St. John Baptist de la Salle.

Where the Church is — there is the Spirit of God.
— St. Irenaeus.

There is no need to seek the truth of others; it is so easy to obtain from the Church. — St. Irenaeus.

Jesus instituted the observance of the divine religion to shed its brightness upon all nations for the salvation of all people. — Pope St. Leo I.

All are called to be members of the Church. — St. Isidore.

It is in the Church that Christ is to be sought. — St. Augustine.

The Church, flooded with the light of the Lord, puts forth its rays through the whole world. — St. Cyprian.

Come together in common, one and all without exception, in charity, in one faith and in one Jesus Christ.
— St. Ignatius of Antioch.

It will remain as long as the sun — the Church of God. — St. Augustine.

If anyone follows a man who causes division in the Church, he does not inherit the kingdom of God. — St. Ignatius of Antioch.

Our faith rests upon the revelation made to the Apostles and preserved by the Church. — St. Thomas Aquinas.

Christ is the head of his body, the Church. . . . — St. Paul (in *Ephesians, Colossians*).

Whoever leaves the Church does not attain the reward of Christ. — St. Cyprian.

There shall be one fold and one shepherd. — Jesus (in *John 10*).

There can be no excuse for destroying the unity of the Church. — St. Augustine.

I should not believe the Gospel except as moved by the authority of the Church. You who believe what you like of the Gospel and believe not what you like, believe yourselves rather than the Gospel. — St. Augustine.

WHAT IS THE MASS?

Do this in memory of me. — Jesus (after the consecration of the Eucharist at the Last Supper, in *Luke*).

When we offer the Sacrifice, be assured that heaven descends to earth, and the angels come among us. — St. John Chrysostom.

We ought to do all things which the Lord has commanded us to perform. — St. Clement of Rome.

Tell the king I am serving a greater king than he. — St. Thomas More (at Mass when a messenger came to tell him that Henry VIII wanted him).

DO THE SACRAMENTS HELP US?
Baptism:

Baptism is the gift of adoption by God, the regeneration of the soul. — St. Basil.

Great is the baptism coming to you — it is ransom to captives and remission of sins. — St. Cyril of Jerusalem.

Penance:

Confession heals; confession grants pardon of sins.
                                — St. Isidore of Seville.

The confession of evil works is the beginning of good works. — St. Augustine.

Confirmation:

It is the custom of the churches for the bishops to journey to those baptized and to impose hands upon them to invoke the Holy Spirit. — St. Jerome.

Anointing the Sick:

If there is anyone sick among you, let him call in the priest and he will anoint him and pray over him. — St. James.

Ordination:

Then, with fasting and prayer, they appointed pastors for them in each of the churches, and commended them to the care of the Lord. — *Acts of the Apostles*.

I remind you to inflame the special grace which God kindled in you, when my hands were laid upon you. — St. Paul (to *Timothy*).

Marriage:

Before all else, invite Christ to your marriage. — St. John Chrysostom.

It is fitting for those who marry that their marriage be according to God. — St. Ignatius of Antioch.

What God has joined together, let no man put asunder. — *Genesis.*

The essential nature of marriage is an indivisible union. — St. Thomas Aquinas.

It is the nursery of Christianity. — St. Francis de Sales.

Therefore a man leaves his father and mother and cleaves to his wife, and they become one flesh.

                                                                — *Genesis.*

Holy Eucharist:

It is good and profitable to receive the Eucharist and partake of the holy Body and Blood of Christ, who clearly says, "He that eats my flesh and drinks my blood has everlasting life." — St. Basil.

The effect of our Communion in the Body and Blood of Christ is that we are transformed into what we have consumed. — St. Leo.

One should show all the reverence and all the honor he possibly can for Christ in the Blessed Sacrament.

                                                        — St. Francis of Assisi.

Give me your grace to long for your Holy Sacra-

ments, and especially to rejoice in the presence of your
very blessed Body — sweet Savior Christ in the Holy Sacrament of the altar — and duly to thank you for your
gracious visitation in that Sacrament at the high memo-
rial of the Mass. — St. Thomas More.

O almighty and eternal God, I approach the Sacrament of your only begotten Son, our Lord Jesus Christ, as
one sick draws near to the Physician of life, as one unclean to the Fountain of mercy, as one blind to the Light
of eternal brightness, as one poor and needy to the Lord
of heaven and earth. . . . I beseech you, grant me not only
to receive the Sacrament of the Body and Blood of the
Lord, but to receive it in all its fullness of grace and vir-
tue. . . . O most loving Father, let me behold this Your
beloved Son, whom I now intend to receive, veiled indeed
in this life, but one day to see him face to face. — St.
Thomas Aquinas.

SHOULD A PERSON FEAR DEATH?

I tell you most solemnly, whoever keeps my word
will never see death. — Jesus (in *John 8*).

Christ rising from the dead dies no more; death shall
no longer have power over him. — St. Paul (in
Romans).

Death is followed by happiness; we die in order to be
with God. — St. Francis de Sales.

What is dying? It is like putting off a garment. — St.
John Chrysostom.

The end of any natural thing cannot be evil. — St.
Thomas Aquinas.

If we have died with Christ, we believe that we are also to live with him. — St. Paul (in *Romans*).

Death is the gate of life. — St. Francis of Assisi.

Praise be my Lord for our sister, death. Death can do no ill. I praise God in my infirmities. I am so united to my Lord that by his mercy I can well now even be merry.
                            — St. Francis of Assisi (when dying).

When the hour comes when earthly life must be lost — we find eternal life with God. — St. Francis Xavier.

WHAT IS ETERNAL LIFE?
We shall enjoy God fully, and all who enjoy Him shall enjoy one another in Him. — St. Augustine.

And God shall wipe away every tear from their eyes: and death shall be no more, nor mourning, nor crying, nor sorrow shall be any more. — *Book of Revelation (Apocalypse)*.

This slight momentary affliction is preparing for us an eternity of glory beyond all comparison. — St. Paul (in *2 Corinthians*).

Come, you blessed of my Father, take possession of the kingdom which has been prepared for you since the foundation of the world. — Jesus (in *Matthew 25*).

Eye has not seen, nor has ear heard, nor has it entered into the mind of man what things God has prepared for those who love Him. — St. Paul (in *1 Corinthians*).

The Risen Christ

For us Christians, Christ is the core and the heart and the center of our religion. To know Jesus is to love him and be loyal to him. We are disciples of the risen Christ. Our Savior lives and is with us here and now.

Christ brought to earth the answers to the mystery of life and death. He told us that love is the way in life and sin a negation of life. His good news, his message of love and hope, shines amid our darkness and warms our sadness.

We poor humans need guidance. And God, because He is good, sent us His Son, so that amid the dust and dullness of our mediocre lives we can have hope. It is for us, day by day, to open our hearts in prayer to the mending love of our divine Guide.

Our days on earth are few, and our minds are clouded; we must hold on to Jesus. It is he who gives us purpose; his words are quiet and soothing to our souls. Where Jesus is, there is tranquillity, even amid our many troubles. With him, the dark clouds are dispersed, sorrows pass, and the sun shines brightly.

Especially when we feel we are coming apart, if we but turn to Christ he will comfort us. This is the testimony of thousands and thousands of Christians. He said, "Come aside with me and rest a while."

SORROW

Jesus understands our pain. He himself was abjectly despised. He knows how we feel in sorrow and gives us spiritual strength. To him, we tiny creatures, no more than grains of sand on the seashore, are very important. As our country grows bigger and more crowded — as we feel more and more like a mere number — Jesus is beside us, especially in troubled times, to help us. His being with us reminds us that although the world ignores us, to God we are of great consequence.

That we are significant in the eyes of our heavenly Father we know from the fact that Jesus died for us. He gathered up his life and gave it to the Father for love of us.

When we place our lives in God's hands, as Jesus did, we are doing the most important thing of all. When we set aside our mulish obstinacy and childish pride and follow Jesus, we are doing what is best for us; we are living our lives as God wishes.

It is so difficult for us to change; we need the help of our Lord daily, hourly. He alone can truly change me. When I lead myself, I go along blindly, bewildered; I must put all my confidence in him, as did the Apostles: "leaving everything, they followed him." Even with him, I don't know where I am going, but I know that if I walk after him I am on the right road and that all — despite trials and hardships — all will work out for the best. In darkness I follow him who is the Light of the world.

PRAYER

The risen Christ is with us. How wonderful that is. We must pray daily to overcome sin, for by sin we drive Christ out of the sanctuary of our souls. Yet, as we know, we cannot pray very well. The main thing is perseverance; we must keep on trying, for as St. Paul tells us, if we pray, the Holy Spirit prays for us. He takes our souls full of human weakness and makes the desert blossom like a rose. He offers up our petitions in a most wondrous way.

PENANCE

Christ, our risen Lord, tells us we must practice penance to overcome our selfishness. Renunciation brings spiritual growth; it removes the obstacles that keep Christ from coming to us. It opens the door of our heart to him and he enters in with great spiritual riches.

Penance helps us to be humble, so that we can grow in love and goodness. God does not reveal himself to the proud; He hides in humble hearts. If we are poor in spirit, the Holy Spirit will invite us quietly along the way to heaven, amid the many ambiguities of life.

Jesus said, "The servant is not greater than his Master." He suffered unpopularity, and if we follow him so shall we. If, with Christ, we go against worldly ways we can expect the same opposition that he had to face. The world did not like Christ because he was otherworldly. Materialists, then and now, cannot stand spiritual people.

Contrary to the notions of the world, Jesus taught that the end of life is not accumulating all the possessions possible; and he taught that those who suffer will reign. He did not try to escape pain, he embraced it. By his life he demonstrated that if one is to overcome evil with good, one must suffer unjustly. Love brings pain, of course, and it is love that makes pain bearable. If a person had never suffered, that person would never have known the joy of real love.

FAITH

"Have mercy on us, Son of David," we cry out with the blind man in the Gospel. Recall that Jesus said to many, "Do you believe?" If we respond, like the father of the mute boy, "I believe — help my unbelief," he will say to us as he said to others, "Your faith has healed you."

It is faith in Jesus that saves us. Jesus said to

Martha, "I am the Resurrection and the Life. . . . do you
believe this?" She answered that she did, and he raised
her brother from the dead. Wherever Christ finds faith,
he refuses nothing. If we have faith, he says to us the
words he addressed to the Roman officer, "Go, and as
you have believed, so be it done to you."

Faith pleases Jesus more than anything. In the
Gospel at times, even when he intended to do nothing,
faith forced him to change his mind. For instance, when
the Canaanite woman called out, "Have mercy . . . my
daughter is grievously troubled," he did not answer her.
In fact, his disciples said, "Send her away; she is bother-
ing us." Jesus explained to her that he had been sent to
the Chosen People, that she was an outsider and, according to the proverb, "One does not take the food from the
children and give it to the dogs."

But her faith would not let go. She cried out, "Even
the dogs get the crumbs that fall from the table." Jesus
was touched by her faith, and he healed her daughter.

Even when he hung in agony on the cross, faith
moved him. The Pharisees had no faith, and he ignored
them. But the thief on his right showed a flicker of faith,
and Jesus pardoned him, enabling the robber to steal
heaven.

Only with faith can we approach Jesus. If we have
faith we will, in the words of Abbot Marmion, "one day
see God unveiled." In heaven we shall see His splendor
as a reward for our faith here on earth.

OUR MODEL

The Father gave us His Son to be our model. Holiness
is making ourselves like Christ. St. John said, "Whoever
has the Son, has life." We should say, "I submit myself to
the Lord." And we should listen to him as if we were with
him person-to-person, face-to-face. St. John wrote, "As

many as received him, he gave the power to be made the sons of God, to them who believe in his name." With Christ we draw abundantly from the divine life, from God's unfathomable riches. In Jesus "are hidden all the treasures of divine wisdom and knowledge."

Christ is always interceding with the Father for us, if we place our unshakable confidence in him. How great and generous he is: he paid all our debts by his death.

What Jesus said in the Gospel is disquieting, for he tells us we must all live together as brothers. It is not easy, but that is what he said. And in our thoughtful moments, we know it is the only way. We will all live together, or we will all perish together.

Jesus not only taught us the way in life, but he died an outcast on the cross for us. All this because each of us is important. After Christ, no man can rightfully use or abuse another man, which was the only way people lived before his coming.

UPSIDE DOWN

Nothing would ever be the same again after Jesus came to earth. He turned the world upside down. Before, most people were slaves, born to serve the high and mighty. Paganism was human rot, but Jesus crushed it completely. To him, not just kings but peasants also had dignity.

The people of Palestine wanted him to lead a revolution. He did. But not the kind they sought. His was not a military revolt, but renewal of mind and heart. He revolted against the old pagan way. The triumph of tyrants had all but ruined the world; his magnificent teachings, however, were the beginning of the end for them. Oh, to be sure, there were other vile and evil kings after Christ came, but men knew in their hearts they were not gods. These devilish figures thereafter might hold power with military might, but they would have to oppose the Light of the world, who reigned in Christian hearts. The poor and deprived found their champion in Christ.

To everyone, Jesus says, "Be not troubled, I am with you. Fear not, peace be to you." In our daily worries and anxieties, he is our hope. In the troubled sea of life, he is the one who rescues us. The invisible Jesus invades our souls and brings love and light and warmth and goodness.

OUR HOPE, OUR HELP

Millions of Christians all over the world and down through the centuries have recited the Our Father. And every time we say it we pray, "Thy kingdom come." We ask God to let the love of heaven fill the world. We know that it must come first to our hearts. When his peace replaces our anguish, when his light guides us, when his courage is so strong in our soul we never lose heart and are never defeated — that is Christ's kingdom coming on earth. With Jesus in our hearts, his love makes us willing to help alleviate human misery. And much of that misery is spiritual, not just physical. The modern pagan thinks only of personal pleasure and entertainment, but the true Christ-follower, with God's help, wishes to make a better world, to spread everywhere on earth the glorious kingdom of love of our Lord Jesus.

THY KINGDOM COME.

The Young Church

How did Jesus ensure that his work would be carried on after he returned to the Father?

Early in his public life he began to plan for the future. He gathered the Apostles around him. They were to be the first leaders and teachers, after he was gone, in his kingdom of love. And so following Pentecost, when they were miraculously enlightened and given courage, the Apostles left Jerusalem and went out to fulfill the final command of Jesus, "Go and tell everyone in the world about me, baptizing them. . . . I am with you always. . . ." They scattered to the four winds preaching the message of Christ. Soon it was known far and wide. This small handful of weak individuals made the good news known, and people accepted it and became Christians by the thousands. Surely this was one of the greatest miracles of all. Christ triumphed with the help of the most unlikely people possible. There is no doubt he had to be with them. He, of course, promised that he would be; he promised he would always be with all of his followers, then and now.

STEPHEN

The authorities in Jerusalem and later in Rome tried to stop this prairie fire. They began to persecute the Christians and murder them. In Jerusalem, a young Christian named Stephen especially attracted attention when he spoke out and told the people about Jesus in a most beautiful way. His words were full of grace and power. He was a deacon. Many of the learned Pharisees and other teachers tried to dispute with him, but "they were not able to withstand the wisdom and the Spirit who spoke," as the author of the Acts of the Apostles relates. It was as if they were dealing with Jesus all over again. And they did the same thing; they could not trap him in debate, so they bribed men to lie about him, and they got together a mob and seized him and brought him before the Sanhedrin.

After the false witnesses told their lies, they let Stephen speak. The young Christian, with the face of an angel, eloquently spoke of Jesus, "The Just One, whom you have betrayed and murdered." The Council was enraged. Stephen looked up to heaven, however, and said that he saw Jesus standing there at the right hand of God.

They rushed at him and took him out of the city and stoned him to death. Stephen had not tried to defend himself. He only prayed, as they started to kill him, with words of love. When he was covered with blood, he still seemed entirely possessed by Christ; with his eyes raised to heaven, he said, "Lord, Jesus, receive my spirit." His last words were, "Lord, do not count this sin against them."

PAUL

One of the young Pharisees who persecuted the early Church with great zeal was Saul. On his way to Damascus to seize some Christians and imprison them, he was knocked from his horse by a great light. He could see nothing as he lay dazed on the ground, but he heard a voice, "Saul, Saul, why do you persecute me?" It is significant that Saul was persecuting the Church but Jesus said he was persecuting *him*.

Saul said, "Who are you, Lord?"

Christ answered, "I am Jesus, whom you are persecuting." Then the Lord told him to go into Damascus.

His companions led him by the hand. There a Christian, Ananias, was called by Christ. The man said, "Here I am, Lord." Jesus told him to go and cure Saul. But Ananias was afraid. Saul was an enemy. The Lord insisted, however, and Ananias at last obeyed. He laid his hands on Saul and the young Pharisee could see. And from that wondrous experience Saul became a Christian with the name of Paul.

His fellow Pharisees were dumbfounded, for he had been one of the most eager among them in trying to stamp out Christianity. They had sent Saul to persecute the Christians, and he had joined them. So now the Pharisees would persecute him. They put guards on the gates of the city to capture him, but he escaped by being lowered in a basket over the wall.

Paul, the new Christian, prayed and wept and wandered — to Arabia, Syria, Cilicia, back to Damascus, Jerusalem, and his native Tarsus. Brought to Antioch by Barnabus, he took part in conversions there and was called by the Lord for a distant errand "to be the light of the Gentiles . . . for salvation to the ends of the earth."

GREAT MISSIONARY

Thus did Paul become the herald of Christ to the non-Jews. To many lands around the Mediterranean Sea, the civilized world at that time, Paul brought the message of divine truth and light.

When Paul faltered, Jesus reassured him, "My grace is enough for you." He endured untold hardship, hunger, cold, betrayal, shipwreck, stoning, but he performed prodigious deeds preaching. Amid his countless crosses, his steadfastness was remarkable. He preached Christ "in season and out of season." He brought faith to a people without faith; in a world that was cynical and skeptical, filled with contradiction, corruption, and covetousness, he told of Christ Jesus, who could make all things right.

GROWTH

The early Church suffered a great deal; in truth, it was great because it suffered. The Romans inflicted untold tortures and even death on the Christians because they would not worship the Emperor. The invisible Christ supported them, however, and they were consoled with his tenderness and so endured. In fact, "the blood of martyrs was the seed of Christianity."

One wonders how people so readily accepted this new message, for Christianity was not easy and paganism permitted almost everything. Christ's followers preached sacrifice and penance and obeying the Ten Commandments. Their teaching turned people away from their evil inclinations to wickedness and inhumanity. In a proud world, Christianity called for humility, so contrary to pagan thinking. Jesus said, "Learn of me for I am meek and humble of heart." In a time when life was cheap, Christianity proclaimed the dignity of man and respect for each individual. Sin ran rampant in Rome and throughout the empire; "might makes right," the law of the jungle, was the rule that prevailed. But these new people repeated what Christ taught — that the greatest individual is the servant of all. "Our humble God," they said, "makes holiness manifest most often in the simple, unlearned people, thereby showing all the more his great power." Every soul reflects the love of God, they said, but the most lowly, humble, and unlikely show it forth even more. Just look at the Apostles!

Holy souls are important, not the high and the mighty who are honored by the world. Christ is with the humble; with them one feels the radiance of his presence. This has been the teaching of Christ, proclaimed by the Church from that time until this.

LIGHT FOR THE WORLD

Christianity was a lighthouse in a world of darkness. The teachings of Jesus brought sanity to an insane world. And the fire that Christ kindled on the earth burned ever more brightly. The Church, the kingdom of love established by Christ, continued to grow and flourish. Many said in the beginning, as they do today, that this was folly and Christians were fools. We should, they said, "eat, drink and be merry, for tomorrow we die." But Christianity from the start answered the inner needs of man, who yearns within for a better world and for eternal life. As St. Augustine said, "Our hearts are restless, O Lord, until they rest in Thee!"

O Blessed Jesus

You are our only life,
  O blessed Jesus dear;
When sorrow comes to us
  Be with us, ever near.

You are our only strength,
  Our hope in time of loss;
We gather, Christ, O Lord,
  Beneath your holy cross.

O Sacred Heart divine,
  O Precious Blood, so pure:
Bless us all each day,
  And help us to endure.

Appendix

Dedication of a Family to the Sacred Heart of Jesus

Bless this home and all who live here. We dedicate our home and family to your Sacred Heart, O Jesus. Please take care of all of us. May we imitate the kindness of your dear Sacred Heart. May there be peace in our home and love and courtesy always. May all strive humbly and sincerely to honor you, Lord Jesus.

Most gentle Lord, our Savior and Redeemer, we are yours, and yours is all we wish to be. We freely give ourselves to your Sacred Heart. Have mercy on us. Bless our loved ones, living and dead. Help us all to draw closer to you, O Christ. Be kind, O Sacred Heart, to all souls, especially to all poor sinners here and the poor souls in purgatory. Give your graces to our relatives and friends, in particular to those most in need.

Wash away our sins, heal our hearts, let there ever be peace in this home and in every heart here. Through the intercession of your loving Mother, please accept our love and dedication. We ask this and beg for your blessings with humble hearts. Amen.

Renewal of the Dedication

Lord Jesus, we place all our trust in your Sacred Heart. We have dedicated our home and family to you, and we are grateful for the many blessings that we have received from your Sacred Heart. So great was your love for us that on the cross there flowed out from your heart blood and water, for our redemption, after the soldier had pierced your side. You love us so much that you emptied yourself for us. You gave everything, you suffered and died, that we might live. We humbly thank you with hearts full of love and appreciation.

Today we rededicate ourselves to you, dear Lord, our good and true Friend. We again give you our family. We know that only with your wondrous blessings can we find peace and happiness. Only with the love of your Sacred Heart can we be protected from evil and grow in grace and goodness. How often you have come to our assistance in our hour of need in the past. In sickness and suffering, in sorrow and trouble, you have been with us, dear Jesus. We could not have endured our hardships and trials without you.

Be with us still. Always be our guest, Jesus. Dwell in our home and in our hearts. Let us have simple faith in you. Help us so that we will not set our hearts on material possessions, but rather will look to you, O Lord.

Bless all we do, divine Heart of Jesus. Bring us peace. Take away our troubles and worries, lighten our burdens, help us in our suffering and sickness; dispel gloom and give joy to our hearts, the joy that only you can give. O Jesus of goodness and mercy, be with us now and always. Amen.

A Prayer for the Family

Dear Jesus, bless our family, here and away, living and dead. Love for us and for all people fills your Sacred Heart. Let your kindness and not anger and hostility reign in our hearts. Be our consolation and comfort in our suffering. May your love be with each of us every day. If you are with us, we do not fear. Help especially the weakest and those most in need of you. We wish you always to be the center of our hearts and home.

Lord Jesus, we give you our family and dedicate each member to you in a most special way. Keep each of us daily in your most Sacred Heart. Amen.